Angler's Mail GUIDE

CATCH BIGGER COARSE FISH

Angler's Mail GUIDE

CATCH BIGGER COARSE FISH

with **Andy Little**

photographs by **Roy Westwood**

EBURY PRESS
LONDON

1 3 5 7 9 10 8 6 4 2

Published in 2007 by Ebury Press, an imprint of Ebury Publishing

A Random House Group Company

Text © Andy Little 2007

Material © IPC Media Limited 2007

Photographs © Roy Westwood 2007

Andy Little has asserted his right to be identified as the author of this Work in accordance with the Copyright, Designs and Patents Act 1988

The Random House Group Limited Reg. No. 954009

Addresses for companies within the Random House Group can be found at www.randomhouse.co.uk

A CIP catalogue record for this book is available from the British Library

The Random House Group Limited makes every effort to ensure that the papers used in our books are made from trees that have been legally sourced from well-managed and credibly certified forests. Our paper procurement policy can be found on www.randomhouse.co.uk

To buy books by your favourite authors and register for offers visit www.rbooks.co.uk

Design by Christine Wood
Project managed by Nikki Sims

Printed and bound in Singapore by Tien Wah Press

ISBN 9780091917906

contents

1 The big-fish scene   6

2 Roach   12

3 Pike   28

4 Barbel   50

5 Tench   70

6 Bream   86

7 Dace   98

8 Crucian carp   108

9 Chub   118

10 Rudd   134

11 Perch   142

12 Carp   154

Index   190
Acknowledgements   192

RIGHT: The syndicate West Stow Lake in Suffolk grows stunning carp, like this 25lb 7oz common.

BELOW: Pike ambush their prey with a short burst of explosive speed and a powerful snap of their ferocious jaws.

1 The big-fish scene

STUNNING INCREASES IN THE SIZE of leading freshwater species means life has never been so good for the UK specimen hunter. Gone are the days when catching big fish consistently meant joining an exclusive syndicate. With careful planning, you can target different species all year round, concentrating your efforts when the conditions are favourable and fish of each species weigh their heaviest. It has become that calculated!

A few years back, nobody would have imagined that we could be looking at the first 70lb carp or targeting 20lb bream and barbel. Even a double-figure chub is surely just around the corner. Good-quality bait and climate change have certainly been contributing factors. On the other side of the coin, species such as rudd, pike, crucian carp and dace are only slowly putting on extra weight – and in some cases none at all. Perhaps they have already reached their growth potential by surviving for longer than other species in those habitats that can fulfil their natural food demands. Who really knows?

More specialist anglers are setting themselves key challenges. Many target several species through the season, rather than limiting their efforts to just one. This trend has been driven by the sheer abundance of big-fish opportunities. Even the secrecy barriers have been lifted since information is now widely available through magazines, such as *Angler's Mail*, and the Internet. Club waters are easily accessible and some of our biggest fish have come from free stretches.

Mobile phones and emails ensure rapid transmission of big-fish news around the country. I've been sitting on the bank of a southern stillwater, speaking to a mate who had just landed the fish of a lifetime in Norfolk. I've even switched waters following a tip received via mobile phone, and caught a monster that I hadn't thought of targeting at the start of the day. The only downside is that some of the mystery has gone from specimen hunting. We are fishing for known specimens rather than gambling on chasing rumours and theories, except when it comes to those species with a short lifespan, such as perch and pike. These predators are still capable of coming through the ranks very quickly and springing surprises. Most huge pike and perch are one-off captures by the speculative angler.

It's no longer necessary to invest in lavish baiting programmes or to spend huge amounts of time on the bank. Track the weather conditions and time your sessions accordingly. If you know the right baits, rigs and location, the rest is down to your own watercraft.

At the top end of the specimen-hunting tree, some anglers set themselves almost impossible challenges. These guys are totally obsessive and happy to forfeit catching plenty of good fish in exchange for a single monster, even though the task might take several seasons to achieve. This is certainly the case in carp and bream fishing, and to some extent it holds true for monster pike.

A famous angler once said that pounds and ounces don't matter. I disagree. For me, and the majority of specialists, accurate documentation is vitally important because it is the yardstick by which personal achievement can be measured. The majority set themselves a defined target that is realistic for the waters they fish and the amount of time at their disposal. When that target is achieved, they set another one for a different species. It's great to look back at your personal bests and compare them against the official British records.

Certain specimens are easier to catch than others. On rivers, a 15lb barbel was previously a pipedream, but now it's achievable. The same goes for a 7lb chub. The stillwater scene has exploded beyond all expectations and 40lb carp no longer cause a ripple. Leading specialists are chasing 50lb carp, which is mind blowing! Big bream appear to be more widespread and a 14-pounder has become the yardstick for most specialists.

For me, a monster roach is the ultimate target – and still one of the hardest to achieve. I have been lucky to catch several 3-pounders from still waters. But if I had to pick one fish as the crowning glory of my angling career, it would have to be a 3lb plus river roach.

The strange thing about big river roach is that they prove impossible to tempt when it's clear and bright, but when it's mild, overcast and the river is high, they'll slurp down big chunks of bread on heavy tackle. These optimum conditions might persist for just a few hours – that's how critical it can be.

Proper documentation of catches is the basis of all specimen hunting and, in this regard, digital scales have helped enormously – with a digital readout, there's no flickering needle to study. I use a highly accurate set of electronic kitchen scales for smaller species, such as dace and silver bream, while larger specimens are recorded on my standard Fox digital scales. Both sets of digital scales weigh in pounds and ounces or kilos. I also have a set of the popular Waymaster scales for a quick initial reading.

Lightweight weigh slings are essential. These should be thoroughly doused with water long before you catch any fish. All the excess water should be wrung out and the sling zeroed on the scales before recording the catch. For accurate reading, the scales must be held perpendicular and away from your body. Any contact could produce a false reading. For large fish, special weigh-bars or a tripod are preferable. It is even better to lash the scales to a large branch instead of trying to support them with shaking hands.

Many anglers also document the length and girth of individual fish because this gives a good guide to weights at specific times of year. A soft plastic, retractable tape is ideal. Most record inches on one side and centimetres on the other. Length is measured from nose to fork of tail since tail length varies dramatically. A good unhooking mat of suitable size for the quarry is essential.

Fish welfare is of prime importance and the aim always is to return the fish as quickly as possible. Some species are best retained in a landing net held in the water to recover before being returned. In rivers, barbel and chub can easily float off downstream and become damaged or wedged in weed-beds. Recently, on the Dorset Stour, a large roach floated past me. I managed to net it and hold it in quieter water for 20 minutes until it recovered and swam away strongly. If that roach had tumbled over a weir downstream, I doubt it would have survived. These days many stillwaters are very heavily weeded and a fish returned too quickly can easily bolt into thick cover. It's better to hold them in the margins and release them only when they look strong enough to swim away. This might take as long as 30 minutes, but the safety of any fish is paramount.

If you are fortunate enough to catch a potential British record, there are strict procedures to follow, and you will require clear photographs, including close-ups of vital areas of identification for tricky species such as roach, rudd and crucians. Take the vital measurements and obtain witnesses to the weighing. The scales must have a weights and measures certificate.

A wealth of knowledge is available to anyone who cares to contact single species groups. Whether your first love is carp, perch or tench, you can meet up with like-minded anglers and share experiences.

Dean Derbyshire of Poole pursued this 11lb barbel on his local Dorset Stour.

RIGHT: Looking every inch a giant in the making, this 1lb 7oz roach from New Forest Water Park at Fordingbridge had the length of a 2-pounder.

BELOW: Casters and hemp are great attractors and tend to be more selective than maggots. Hemp is often used with a larger tare seed on the hook to avoid small fish.

2 Roach

I F YOU RELISH A SERIOUS COARSE-FISHING challenge, line up a big, suspicious roach as your next target. All types of waters throughout the UK hold genuine heavyweights, but they are among the toughest species to deceive. As roach grow older and heavier they become correspondingly wiser and reject anything that smacks of danger.

Past surveys flagged up roach as the nation's favourite species and I'd guess that is still true, despite the carp's cult following. The reason for the species' enduring popularity is not purely down to its widespread distribution. The roach, with its silver body and bright red fins, also qualifies as one of the handsomest of freshwater fish. For me, it represents the classic shape of a native coarse fish.

Roach thrive in weedy farm ponds, wind-blown lowland reservoirs, major rivers and trickling brooks. They may be taken all year round, but larger specimens are usually caught during winter floods, when coloured water helps mask the tackle. Big roach are Jekyll and Hyde characters, showing extreme wariness one minute and sudden greed the next. They shy away from the finest rigs in clear, calm conditions, yet after dark it's not unusual for them to gulp down carp anglers' boilies on heavy tackle. Their sharp eyesight makes them virtually impossible to catch on sunny days. I've often watched big roach confidently snatch free offerings in clear water but totally ignore baits on tiny hooks and low-diameter lines.

This glorious roach of 2lb 14oz 8dr came from Sway
Lakes in the New Forest where Andy has taken many
notable redfins – including a personal best fish of 3lb 7oz.

WEIGHT AND LIFE EXPECTANCY

Roach weighing 2lb have long been the target for most specimen hunters, although the British record stands at 4lb 5oz. Two-pounders are highly prized while a 3-pounder is the fish of a lifetime. Realistically, you are unlikely ever to come across a 4-pounder. The species is very slow growing and most roach are no more than 4 or 5in. long by their third year. They have been known to survive for 20 years, but life expectancy is probably nearer 15.

Stillwater roach have learned to capitalise on carp baits scattered into gravel pits and lakes and, as a result of feeding on these nutritious boilies and pellets, tend to fatten up faster than their river cousins. That makes it much easier to catch a 2lb roach from a lake than a river. Some of the most consistent big-roach fishing is to be found on carp-dominated pits.

In contrast, river fishing is frequently deeply frustrating, but when you do finally catch a 2lb roach from running water, the sense of achievement is that much greater. In rivers, big roach are notoriously finicky feeders. They are often visible in summer, drifting in and out of the weed-beds, delicately picking up morsels from the clean gravels.

A distinct pecking order exists within a roach shoal. Smaller fish congregate at the front while larger, nervous specimens hold back downstream. It's almost as if the bigger fish watch what the juveniles are doing and carefully select the odd freebie that drifts down to them. Sometimes, you'll find a small shoal of maybe six very large roach that have broken away to seek a more solitary existence. In my experience, these breakaway groups are the ones to target.

In certain conditions, however, river roach become far more catchable. The magic forecast is a mild winter's day when the river is carrying plenty of colour and a few extra inches of water. Raging floods spoil the prospects of success. On those rare days when the conditions are spot on, I drop everything and head for the river.

The Dorset Stour fining down after a recent flood. Now the weed has died back it's possible to trot an Avon float and breadflake through the roach holding spots.

TACTICS FOR LOW, CLEAR RIVERS

Summer river fishing demands fine match tackle with hemp, casters and tares. My basic set-up is a 13ft match rod, free-running centrepin reel and 2lb reel line. Floats are usually wire-stemmed Avons or sticks. I use a tiny, No. 20 micro swivel to attach a low-diameter hook link of around 0.10mm. The link is normally clear and low stretch. A fine-wire, spade-end hook completes the set-up.

I use hemp as the main attractor, feeding little and often to generate competitive feeding among the shoal. Hook baits are single or double casters, but if I'm plagued by bait-robbing minnows, I switch to a single tare. The choice between single and double casters is dictated by water clarity. When rivers run crystal clear and low, I bury the whole hook inside a single caster. Roach have such keen eyesight that they can actually see a hook outside the caster. Double casters are slightly more selective if there is extra pace and colour in the river, or when light levels are low.

It's possible to stalk individual fish using similar tactics with the help of a longer float rod or pole. Using a 19ft float rod, I can carefully manoeuvre a stubby pole float, fished on the lightest line possible, through the swim into the path of a big fish.

A good alternative is to touch leger with a single shot to hold bottom. In the right conditions, you can watch a big roach pick up your hook bait. Choose a heavily weeded swim with small, clear runs and, if you wear Polaroid sunglasses, you should be able to observe big roach ghosting in and out of the weed. Good control of the tackle is critical because the hook bait must look as natural as possible. In summer, many of the biggest roach are caught by this method.

At this time of year, too, roach lose their caution after dark. If you pack a small, block-end feeder with hemp and casters, you'll get plenty of bites on a light quivertip rod fitted with a small betalight.

BAITS AND RIGS IN WINTER FLOODS

On rivers, it's all change in the winter months, especially after the first floods have ripped out the weeds. Look for deep, steady glides with a uniform depth, and avoid boiling water, uneven bottoms and fluctuating depths. Long trotting is usually the most productive method.

Casters still work if the water is clear, but sometimes breadpunch is even better. With no colour in the water, I feed a finely sieved groundbait of pure white bread. It should be just damp enough to stick together in a ball when compressed in the palm of your hand. This consistency ensures it will break up into thousands of particles as it drifts downstream. Breadpunch under a stick float is a killing combination in these conditions.

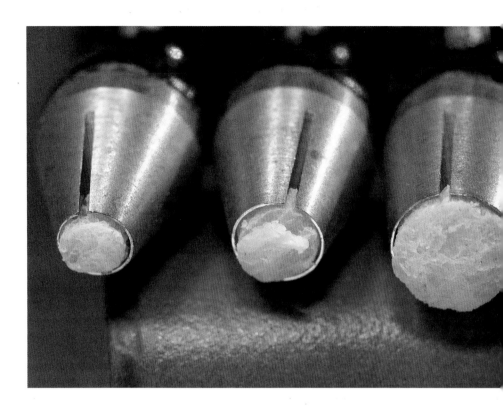

Punched white bread – the right formula for a clear river in winter.

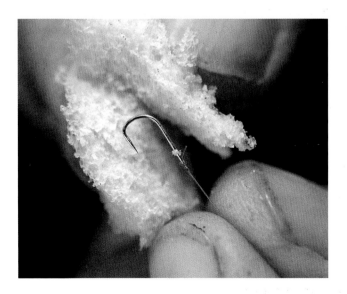

Think big at flood-time and increase the bait size to a ragged chunk of flake on the hook.

When the river floods, use the same rod and reel but rig up larger floats carrying several swanshot. There is no better bait for floodwater roach than a big piece of flake torn from a fresh, thick-sliced loaf. This must be fished close to the bottom, and it might require as many as five swanshot to get it down to the right depth. Buoyant balsa bodies or clear plastic Chubber-like patterns are suitable for this style of fishing.

I still use a tiny swivel between the main line and hook link, but all the bulk shot are grouped directly above the swivel. I place a single dropper shot halfway along the hook link, which is 6–9in. long.

For groundbait, soak half a loaf of bread in a bucket of water. Mash it up by hand and feed tangerine-sized balls at the head of the swim. Squeeze the groundbait into tight balls to get it down or feed a more sloppy consistency so it quickly breaks up into smaller particles, depending on the depth and the speed of the current.

Once again, the biggest winter specimens lurk at the rear of the shoal. To select these fish, cast a little farther downstream before you start the trot. Smaller roach often move right up to where the groundbait lies, and settle beneath the rod tip. Casting downstream allows you to trot your bait directly towards the bigger fish. It is possible to trot roach swims 40 yards downstream. Bites from the biggest fish should come at the end of the trot – the float may be dragged under, almost like snagging the bottom. I prefer thumbnail-sized pieces of flake on a size 12 hook. Hold the float back at times, so the flake flutters up a few inches. The reaction is often a positive bite that's felt right through the rod – a total contrast to the delicate dips of the float in the summer.

COMPETITIVE FEEDING ON LAKES

Stillwater roach fishing involves a wide range of tactics, largely driven by the size of the water. Basic float rigs are all that's needed on the small, intimate carp lakes that produce monster roach. In summer, nothing beats 'wag and mag', a method for shallow venues where the roach shoal at relatively short range. Continually spraying maggots at 25 yards is a great way to create competitive feeding. I often catapult bait for the first ten minutes of a session before rigging up a waggler to fish on the drop. A loaded waggler with a fine insert tip casts well, provides stability and registers the most delicate bites.

In water that is less than 3ft deep, I bulk all the shot around the base of the float and let the hook bait fall naturally. Bites are likely at any depth. But increasing the feed rate tempts the roach to rise higher in the water. I find two maggots on a size 18 fine-wire hook and 2lb line straight through is perfect for 'wag and mag' fishing.

Drennan's loaded Crystal Tip peacock wagglers are a sound choice for stillwater roach. The insert tips are interchangeable for varying light conditions and they are fitted with quick-change attachments at the base.

Bulk most of the shot around the base for tangle-free presentation. Leave a gap between the locking shot so that the float lays flat against the line when striking.

The coloured water in small, heavily stocked carp lakes means roach are less tackle shy, but overcast days with a slight wind are still preferable to bright sun and flat calm. On some waters, you may need to fish close against the far bank, or an island. To prevent the rig being pulled out of position, you must sink the line between rod tip and waggler. I degrease the spool of line the previous night by soaking it in a diluted mixture of washing-up liquid and water. I also take a film canister filled with the same mix and a scrap of sponge to degrease the line during the session. A small fixed spool and standard 13ft match rod are all you require for this method.

In places where small fish are a nuisance, I substitute pellets or mini boilies for maggots. Soft pellets can be attached directly to the hook, hard pellets are banded to the shank and mini boilies are side-hooked. These very selective roach baits work well in carp waters.

In winter, baits need to be nailed hard on the bottom. Casters and hemp sink quickly and can be grouped into a small area to concentrate the feed. Smaller silver fish are less of a nuisance in cold conditions, so scale down the gear and fish a single caster on a light hook link. Use the same loaded waggler but with several dropper shot on the hook link for stability. I fish slightly over-depth with at least one shot on the bottom, because big roach will not tolerate bait skidding through in the undertow. Watch out for lift bites as the roach delicately suck in the caster and momentarily lift the bottom shot, making the float rise in the water.

I try to arrive on the bank before first light to locate a shoal of big roach. They roll on the surface at daybreak and are unlikely to move far in cold conditions. Expect bites at both ends of the day in low light levels and, if you can, fish on for a couple of hours after dark with a chemical light fitted to the top of your float. There is nothing more exciting than a Starlite disappearing into the inky blackness.

LOCATING ROACH ON BIG GRAVEL PITS

In the UK, large, clear gravel pits produce some of the biggest specimen roach. Again, these venues tend to be carp waters, but usually lightly stocked. Roach of 3lb are known to rub shoulders with 40lb carp. Location is tricky – roach rolling at daybreak and dusk give the clearest clues but these fish are very nomadic. They rarely patrol the margins, preferring deep areas where the bottom is clean and level.

In this environment, winter nearly always produces better roach fishing than other times of the year for two reasons. One is that carp are more active in

The wind dies at dusk making it much easier to spot large roach rolling across the lake on a mirror-like surface.

summer and push the roach out of baited swims. The other is that roach shoals split up in warmer weather and are more evenly distributed throughout the gravel pit. As temperatures fall, the size of the shoals increases, and they don't move far until the water warms up again in April or May, when they head for the shallows to spawn. Traditionally, monster roach are hooked in March when the females are at their heaviest.

A typical gravel-pit roach swim is 10–15ft deep, with a clear bed, at a range of 30–70 yards. Islands and bars may look very appealing on first inspection but are usually frequented by carp, which soon hustle away any roach shoals.

Long casting with paternoster rigs at Catch 22 in Norfolk has produced many headline roach.

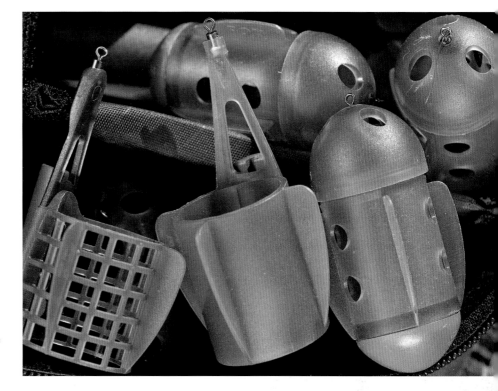

Big lake roach have inspired specialist paternoster rigs featuring fluorocarbon main line, short hook links and feeders that fly to the horizon. Use cage feeders for explosive groundbaits and solid open-enders to trap large pellets and particles between plugs of groundbait. Block-ends are ideal for maggots.

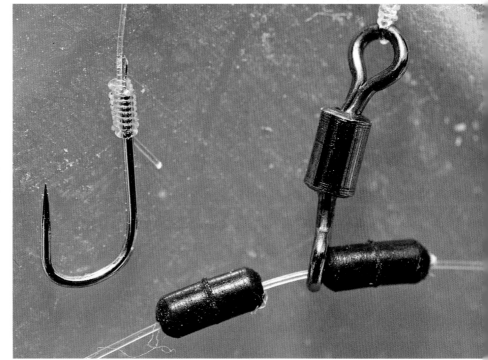

Short hook links are rigged helicopter style with a micro swivel trapped between braid stops. Hook choice on this rig was a Kamasan B611 to carry two maggots.

TACTICS ON GRAVEL PITS

Feeder fishing is the core tactic on gravel pits. I break my approach down into three categories: maggots with a block-end feeder, bread using a cage feeder, and mini boilies and pellets with a solid open-end feeder. In each case, I use fluorocarbon main line and hook links, because fluorocarbon has minimal stretch and is virtually invisible in water, sinking like a stone. The three methods have different configurations.

I fish the maggot feeder paternoster-style, and use two hooks where permitted. These are tied on 4in. hook links trapped between two rig stops, which allows them to be fixed at varying distances on the main line above the feeder. I use a size 20 fine-wire pattern for a single maggot or an 18 for two.

For the bread rig, I normally go for a sliding cage feeder and a hook link of between 1 and 2ft, depending on how the fish are feeding. For groundbait, finely sieved white bread is my choice, dampened to hold together and tightly packed in the cage feeder so that it explodes out as it takes on water. The hook bait is a thumbnail-sized piece of flake squeezed over a size 12.

For the third method, I fish a solid open-end feeder semi-fixed with a 6–9in. hook link, and have a mini boilie or pellet fixed on a very short hair to a size 18, eyed hook. Pellets or mini boilies are trapped in the middle of the feeder between plugs of groundbait.

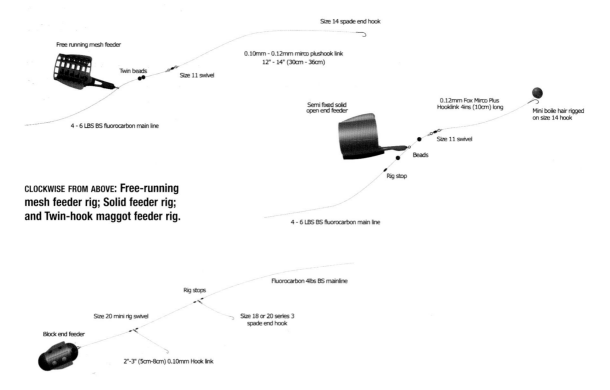

Free running mesh feeder

Twin beads

Size 11 swivel

Size 14 spade end hook

0.10mm - 0.12mm mirco plushook link
12" - 14" (30cm - 36cm)

4 - 6 LBS BS fluorocarbon main line

Semi fixed solid
open end feeder

0.12mm Fox Mirco Plus
Hooklink 4ins (10cm) long

Mini boilie hair rigged
on size 14 hook

Size 11 swivel

Beads

Rig stop

4 - 6 LBS BS fluorocarbon main line

CLOCKWISE FROM ABOVE: Free-running mesh feeder rig; Solid feeder rig; and Twin-hook maggot feeder rig.

Fluorocarbon 4lbs BS mainline

Rig stops

Size 20 mini rig swivel

Size 18 or 20 series 3
spade end hook

Block end feeder

2"-3" (5cm-8cm) 0.10mm Hook link

I usually use 4lb main line with a 2lb hook link, but for really long-range casting, I might attach an 8lb shock leader, also of fluorocarbon, to punch out a heavy feeder. Small, free-spool reels are perfect for the method and I like to use a 12ft specimen rod with a half-pound test curve tip. This rod is less likely to cause hook pulls than a heavy duty, barbel-type model, which, with a fine-wire hook, exerts too much pressure on a big fish. Depending on the water, I fish two or three rods with buzzers and bobbins, positioning the rods low to the water. The indicators are ultra-light and the lines fairly slack.

After locating a roach shoal, I bait up a tight area with the feeder contents in swims less than 10ft deep or spod out freebies. In deeper water, I cast out a baitdropper that will jettison its load on contact with the bottom. Accuracy is essential to build up a tight bed of bait, and a brightly coloured marker braid attached to the line guarantees that I cast to the same spot every time. Line up the cast with a marker on the far bank to get the trajectory right. At night, select a prominent silhouette on the horizon.

I prefer to put down one big bed of bait at the start of the session, and top up with the feeder, which I sometimes leave in place for several hours between casts. Gravel-pit roach need time to start feeding confidently over a bed of bait and this is more likely to happen at night, especially in clear water.

The amount of bait to put down is set by the venue. Some roach shoals are huge while others contain just a handful of fish. Get to know the water and bait up accordingly. At some venues, I introduce a mere half a pint of free offerings while on others a couple of pints around each rod are the starting point.

Most action occurs at night, and it's rare to experience screaming runs or self-hooked fish. I sit over the rods and strike at any positive movement of the indicator. Once you've had one bite, expect more in quick succession. It's far better to hover over the rods than doze in the bedchair.

Slack lines and light bobbins magnify twitch bites from big roach.

RIGHT: River pike don't come much better than this. Andy's 34lb 7oz monster was hooked from the Barton Court beat on the upper Kennet near Hungerford. The £1,000 a year brown trout fishery opens for day ticket coarse fishing in winter and that's when Andy slipped in and followed up a tip from manager Bob Bailey that a big pike was in residence.
(Photo: Greg Meenehan/*Angler's Mail*)

BELOW: All these blow-moulded river floats make excellent sliders. The fluted models are particularly stable for trotting in flow or for float paternoster rigs.

3 Pike

THE PIKE IS ONE OF THE FEW coarse fish to qualify as a true native of the British Isles. Fossil experts say our top predator was active in Eastern England 500,000 years ago. A 20-pounder, which is less than half the British record weight, remains the target for all specialists. Most waters are capable of producing double-figure fish, but specimens over 30lb are rare.

Pike are fast growing, easily reaching 8lb in their third year, and well-stocked trout lakes and reservoirs are capable of producing 20-pounders within five years. Life expectancy is short: pike might survive 15 years in lightly fished, naturally stocked waters but this is halved on trout lakes, where they are exposed to heavy angling pressure.

Specimen pike may be captured in the most unlikely places. Massive fish have been taken from tiny bagging pools after gorging on a diet of hand-sized carp. Game-fishing beats on chalk streams provide a potentially pampered lifestyle for big pike, because the fish can hunt unmolested. Pike will tolerate brackish water and big fish emerge in tidal estuaries, where they survive on a mixed diet of coarse and sea fish.

The most predictable pike waters, though, are trout reservoirs, where annual growth rates of 7lb have been recorded. But this spectacular weight gain comes at a price: reservoir monsters are prone to heart failure and die young.

Chunky 20lb 12oz Kennet pike hooked at first light on a sardine at Barton Court. Trout waters historically produce fast-growing pike and the upper Kennet is no exception.

UNHOOKING PIKE

Despite their ferocious image, pike are fragile. They need careful handling, and treble-hook rigs are difficult to remove from a mouthful of teeth and razor-sharp gill rakers. Responsible fishing clubs insist that novices attend pike teach-ins to ensure confident and safe handling, and with that experience it is quite possible to unhook pike quickly, without damage. Long-handled forceps, pliers, side-cutters and an unhooking mat are essential, and it's advisable to wear a glove, especially with small pike that gyrate on the wire trace.

When the pike has been landed, lay it on its back on a wet unhooking mat and kneel astride the fish, supporting it between your knees. Slip one hand carefully under the gill cover to grip the bottom jaw and pull it away from the rigid, fixed top jaw. This keeps the pike's mouth wide open, allowing you to remove the hooks with long forceps. If the hooks are towards the back of the throat, pass the forceps through the gill rakers for easier access, and lock on to one of the bends. A gentle rotating movement of the forceps will free the hook. Semi-barbed trebles help with unhooking because they have two barbless hooks and just one bait-retaining barb.

NATURAL DIET

The pike is the ultimate ambush predator. It lies motionless near the bottom, often among weeds, where its mottled body markings provide superb camouflage. The dorsal, anal and tail fins are grouped together and act like a giant propeller to give the fish rapid acceleration as it explodes like a sprinter out of the blocks to seize its prey with a short-lived burst of speed.

The pike strikes forward and up because its eyes are located high on its head. Juvenile pike rely totally on eyesight when hunting while mature fish use all their sensory organs. As well as having a keen sense of smell, large pike are able to detect vibrations from prey. These senses become more acute with age.

Some big pike are exclusively nocturnal feeders, especially on large, open gravel pits where bream are their chief fodder. Bream are night feeders, possibly because they feel safer in reduced visibility, and this may influence the pike's habits. In daylight, bream shoals cruise near the surface, which makes them difficult for pike to catch. Try a night session to test out this theory rather than heading home at dusk.

Pike capitalise on whatever food is available, a fact that should be born in mind when selecting baits. Large lures simulating trout work well in trout reservoirs, for instance. On gravel pits, pike might feed once a week only, preying on larger species, such as bream, and on these waters large deadbaits may be successful. In other waters, pike may be preoccupied with

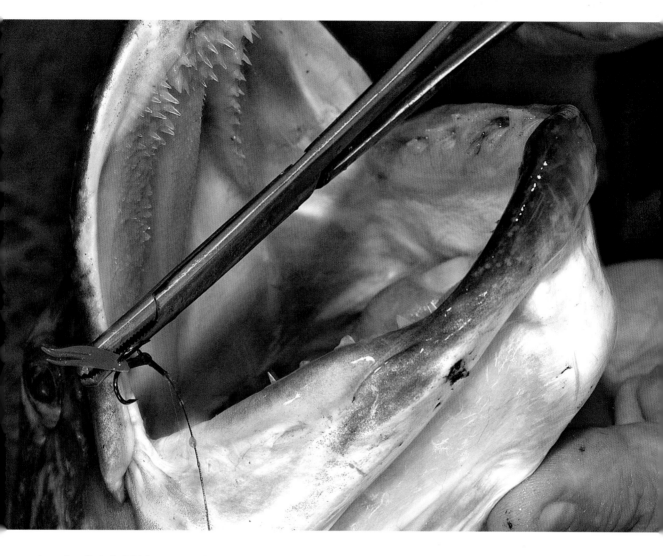

Long-handled straight forceps or pliers are critical for safe treble removal from a pike, which is best laid on its back on a wet unhooking mat. Sit astride the fish to keep it still and grip the bottom jaw through the gill. This should open the jaws, exposing the hooks.

fry. I've landed numerous pike that have regurgitated dozens of tiny fry in the landing net. Huge pike have been caught on tiny baits barely a couple of inches in length. Keep an open mind on bait choice and remember that biggest is not always best.

INSTANT TAKES OVER HOTSPOTS

On certain waters, pike fishing is restricted to the traditional winter period from October 1 to March 14. Often the reason given is the vulnerability of summer pike, but I find that during these months the fish are leaner, fight a lot harder and recover faster. I always return them as quickly as possible, whatever the time of year. For me, action-packed river piking with lures is particularly absorbing in summer.

Brooding sky on the
Kennet at Barton Court
warns of imminent bad
weather. Andy is just
seconds away from
hooking a 20-pounder
in the dark pool.

Pike spawn towards the end of the traditional season, in mid-March, or slightly earlier in the south. The heaviest pike are usually taken just before spawning when the females are swollen with ripe eggs. Once preoccupied with spawning, they prove extremely difficult to catch, and I tend to hang up my pike rods until the end of June, giving them ample time to recover and start feeding aggressively.

Big pike are among the easiest fish to catch and, if you choose the right place, it's not unusual to get a take from a monster within seconds of casting, especially on rivers. The knack is to find a spot where a big pike is lying up. Pike cover huge distances in some waters, shadowing shoals of prey fish, but in others, instead of burning energy chasing food, they take up residence in one spot and rely on passing trade.

It helps to take note of what any pike in the vicinity are feeding on, which may sound obvious but this basic principle tends to be overlooked. Spotting shoals of prey fish is time consuming but worth the effort. In winter, look for them near the surface at dawn and dusk. Fry often congregate in the same areas each year – locate these and pike won't be far away. Fish-eating birds, such as grebes and cormorants, also provide clues to the location of the pike's prey. With binoculars, you may even be able to see exactly what the birds are eating. Grebes gang up to work areas that have large concentrations of fish, and it's odds on that pike will be there, too.

On big rivers, flooding may force shoals of prey fish to seek sanctuary in lock cuttings, flood relief channels and backwaters, and pike follow them. Marinas are one of the best pike hotspots on navigable rivers because dense shoals of roach and bream stream into the slack water from the main river.

On lakes and gravel pits, look for gravel bars, drop-offs, deep gulleys and islands, all of which attract pike. Add reed-beds, dying lily pads, wooden stagings and piers and you've got plenty of spots to target. It's rare to find pike in open water where the depth is uniform because they rely on concealment and camouflage to ambush their prey.

Match anglers usually know of areas where pike repeatedly snatch hooked fish, but remember that you will not be alone in your investigations. Specialist pike anglers are constantly checking reports of pike activity. I like to find my own pike rather than following in someone else's footsteps. It provides a much greater sense of achievement.

The first deadbait to break water at first light often pulls the best pike of the day. Andy swings out a sardine with eager anticipation on the upper Avon at Salisbury.

CHOICE OF BAIT

There are three types of bait for pike – livebait, deadbait and lures. Livebaits produce more pike than any other method, where permitted. You can buy them at some venues, at others you must catch your own from the same water. There are restrictions on the number and size of baits you can retain in a single day, and byelaws prohibit any movement of livebait between waters, principally to prevent the spread of disease.

The problem with livebaits is that they are the least selective of all the methods. Eight inches is usually the maximum length, and they'll attract pike from 2 to 20lb. I'd say you are more likely to catch smaller pike on livebaits, because young pike are mainly sight feeders.

Pike readily accept sea deadbaits. Mackerel, herring, sardines and sprats probably account for most pike nationwide, purely because they are convenient – they can be bought at fishmongers and supermarkets – and acceptable at most venues. Specialist bait firms supply plenty of alternatives, including smelt, lamprey, eels, trout and pollan. I'd say the most productive deadbait for big pike is a headless mackerel, 6in. in length.

If sea fish are rejected, try roach, rudd, perch or skimmer bream. Trout are also effective as deadbaits, but they don't appeal to pike on all waters. Most

Oily mackerel tail with one treble in the tough tail root and the other halfway along the shank – the best positions for an instant strike. Size 8 trebles are big enough on carbon-coated stainless-steel leader, which is easy to tie or crimp.

pike anglers carry a selection of sea and freshwater deadbaits and vary them until one proves acceptable to the pike on the day.

Lures were once regarded as a method of last resort, but attitudes have changed. Now some specialist pike anglers use them exclusively, claiming lures are more successful than live or deadbaits. I have great confidence in lures when conditions dictate they should be used. Their popularity was boosted by trout reservoirs banning both live and deadbaits. Some reservoirs also insist that lures must be over 6in. in length, which is far longer than patterns normally sold in tackle shops.

The result of all this was a revolution in UK lure fishing, influenced by American muskie anglers and spearheaded by the now infamous jerk baits – large chunks of painted wood crafted to mimic wounded fish when pulled through the water with a downward jerking motion on the end of a short, stiff rod. These baits soon sparked interest in soft rubber lures, moulded into fish shapes with lifelike colouring. Pike find their natural texture very appealing.

Although massive lures are used on reservoirs, I favour much smaller versions between 2in. and 4in. long. Mini, wooden-style jerk baits, as well as soft rubber ones and even hybrids of the two, have become a vital component of my revitalised lure fishing kit for fast growing reservoir pike.

Runt, Dolphin, Moocher and Rooter – there's a mass of eye-catching jerkbaits. But to get them working correctly they must be fished on a stiff-actioned 6 or 7ft rod and a solid, single strand trace.

RIGS FOR LIVEBAITING

Most of my livebaiting is done with a slider float, held at the correct depth by a bead and stop-knot. The main patterns for roving-style bait are Slimline, Stubby and Livebait sliders. Shorter, stubbier floats are better for larger baits and fast-running swims that demand extra buoyancy. Slimmer models are fine with smaller baits or when trotting downstream in a steady current.

Although the size and shape of the float varies, the set-up is very similar. A wire trace, constructed of 20 or 30lb Carboflex wire, is my preferred hook-link material. I normally make hook links 15–20in. long and use one or two semi-barbed treble hooks, depending on bait size. I use a quality, size 6 or 8 carbon treble for most of my pike fishing in open water.

All my treble hooks carry a coloured bait flag on the barbed prong. The flag is attached after the hook has been pulled through the skin of the bait, and helps to hold the hook in place. Flags also act as attractors and help to induce takes, but the main reason for using a flag is to identify the barbed hook in low light.

I crimp both trebles and a size 7 swivel on to the wire trace and the method has never let me down. The main line is usually floating braid between 20 and 30lb, which gives good presentation and, unlike standard mono, doesn't need

BELOW LEFT: Paternoster sunk float rig.

BELOW: Drifter set-up.

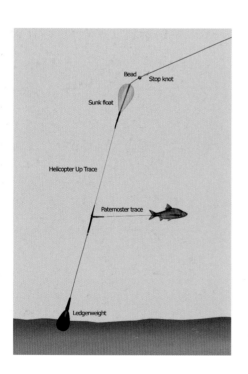

Bead
Stop knot
Sunk float
Helicopter Up Trace
Paternoster trace
Ledgerweight

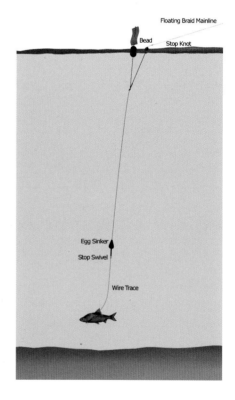

Floating Braid Mainline
Bead
Stop Knot
Egg Sinker
Stop Swivel
Wire Trace

Crimped, semi-barbless treble with a red flag on the single, micro-barbed hook. It quickly identifies the bait-holding hook in low light.

continually treating with floatant to stop it sinking. An Egg sinker that has a rubber tube extension to push over the swivel and hold it semi-fixed completes the rig.

Another effective rig for livebaiting is the sunken paternoster, which is cast tight against a feature, for instance an island, and left in place. A leger weight ensures that the rig doesn't shift and a buoyant, sunk float keeps the set-up perpendicular in the water so the livebait can move around naturally on a helicopter-style presentation. I use a shorter hook trace of 12–14in. and make both the uptrace and leger link 20in. long. Using 20 or 30lb Carboflex wire ensures that you don't get bitten off should the pike swim through the upper trace on the take. I prefer to position the hooks so that the bait is always swimming away from the rig. To do this, fix the upper hook in the root of the tail and the end hook just in front of the dorsal fin. This rig can be used with electronic and visual forms of bite indication.

Two free-roving set-ups are useful. For the drifter rig, the normal float is replaced with one that has a vaned top, which allows you to sail the rig on the wind across large expanses of water. I'm also keen on the in-line troller for boat fishing. This float automatically locks in place to prevent it sliding down towards the bait when pulled along behind the boat.

TREBLE POSITIONS FOR INSTANT-STRIKE RIGS

My thinking about hooking arrangements has changed over time. I believe that a pike grabs its prey across the flanks, then turns it to eat headfirst. So what about a half or headless sea fish, and long, thin baits such as eels and lamprey? Having watched pike eating live eels, I'm not sure the headfirst theory applies on all occasions. I was fascinated to watch a 15lb pike snatch a 1lb plus eel halfway along its length and swim around for 15 minutes with the eel clamped in its jaws. It finally swallowed the eel middle first with the head and tail sticking out either side of the jaw.

Most anglers try to create instant-strike rigs to avoid deep hooking pike, but the frustration of missed fish often persuades them to let a take develop for longer, which is the wrong response. For stillwaters, position one treble just in front of the dorsal fin and the second at the root of the pectoral fin. In running water, the upper treble goes through the top lip of the livebait while the end treble is fixed in front of the anal fin. These set-ups constitute instant-strike rigs that virtually guarantee the pike is hooked in the scissors without any need to allow the take to develop.

WOBBLING TACTICS AND SENSITIVE PENCIL RIGS

For deadbaiting, I adopt two different approaches, one with static and the other with moving bait. Retrieving a deadbait is known as wobbling. For this, exactly the same trace is used as for livebaiting, but with a slightly larger front treble or single hook, to secure the bait at the head. The hook is passed through both lips and a bait flag pushed down over the barb to stop the bait bouncing off on the cast. The end treble is fixed close to the anal fin, sometimes under slight tension to bend the bait and induce more movement on the retrieve.

With this method, I prefer a fluorocarbon main line, which is virtually invisible in the water, sinks quickly and offers good abrasion resistance. To provide extra casting and sinking weight, large swanshot can be fixed in front of the swivel and adjusted according to depth and retrieve.

The bait is simply cast out and allowed to sink to the bottom before being slowly and erratically wound back to mimic an injured fish. It's worth pausing the retrieve and fishing the bait static for a few seconds because this can induce a strike. Since you are continually casting and retrieving, you need tough bait. Roach or rudd are my first choice, followed by smelt or trout. Wobbling is highly productive on rivers and stillwaters and is excellent for covering a lot of water.

For the static approach, I generally use either a float or a straight leger set-up. For float fishing, I prefer to use a deadbait pencil or loaded lift deadbait float. Again, the same hook trace is used and an Egg sinker, fished semi-fixed with the

Fluttering a pike deadbait between rafts of loose weed trapped in a large eddy on the Royalty's top weirpool.

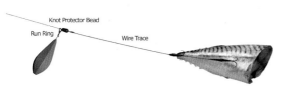

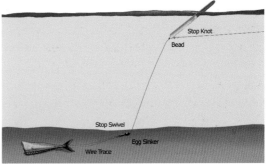

ABOVE: **Deadbait leger rig.**

RIGHT: **Deadbait pencil float set-up.**

rubber pushed over the eye of the swivel. Ideally, the deadbait pencil should be fished slightly over-depth and the line sunk between the rig and rod top. I keep the line tensioned using a line clip or drop-off indicator with an open bale arm.

A fluorocarbon main line makes sense because it's far easier to sink than other material, and unobtrusive. With the line held slightly under tension, the deadbait pencil float should cock at a slight angle. It dives straight under on a take, or more often lays flat on the surface as the pike picks up the bait and dislodges the weight. This method suits all deadbaits and is a very effective instant-strike rig.

A slight variation is achieved with a loaded lift deadbait pencil, which is self-cocking. It can be used in the same way as the standard pencil but is far more sensitive and causes less resistance. This rig comes into its own when takes are tentative in low water temperature. You should strike immediately the float moves up or down.

For longer-range fishing or in running water, I use a static leger deadbait rig. This is probably the simplest set-up of all, comprising a twin treble trace between 18 and 20in. in length with a free-running leger weight attached to a run ring and stopped. The ring has a very large, lightweight eye that greatly reduces any resistance that might be felt by a taking pike. Once again, I use fluorocarbon main line, and I normally place the rod on a couple of rests and attach a bite indicator.

RIGHT: Wobbling a dead roach through a sheltered weedy bay on Gingerbread Lake in Cambridgeshire.

BELOW: Pencil deadbait floats register the most delicate of pick-ups by lifting up or falling flat on the surface, depending on whether the float is loaded or unloaded.

Single-hook kebab rig with chunks of deadbait mounted on a hair-rig. The flavour leak-off is terrific.

KEBAB RIG

I've had great success with another variation on the deadbait theme called the kebab rig, which mimics a carp hair-rig. Chunks of cut fish are mounted on a hair hanging from a single hook. This rig leaks potent juices and smells far more quickly than uncut baits. It casts a lot farther and, to my mind, the single hook has greater conservation appeal than a set of trebles. It's important to keep the hair quite short with the bait touching the bend of the hook. This allows an instant strike and usually results in the pike being hooked in the corner of the mouth.

All sorts of baits are suitable for this method, but my favourites are chunks of sardine for short range and mackerel for long range. The rig is very flexible and you can use as many chunks of fish as you like. I normally cut mine into 1in. sections and fish one piece with a size 1 hook and up to six chunks with a size 4/0. You require a large hair stop to keep the baits in place and I've found that a luncheon meat stop is by far the best. I also add a float stop to the hair, so that the bait is held tightly between the float and luncheon meat stops. This is especially useful for long-range fishing.

One good trick with the kebab rig is to catapult similar-sized chunks of fish around the rig to inject more smell and flavour into the water, drawing the pike towards the bait. Using a Method-style catapult, you can fire a semi-frozen chunk of mackerel 80 yards.

SUSPENDED BAIT

Whether I present deadbaits on the bottom or suspended just above it depends on the swim. Suspended bait is the better option in some conditions, so it's worth experimenting. For instance, where weed and debris are in abundance, I find it best to present the bait just clear of the bottom. To add buoyancy, insert

The bait popper has its own 9in. long wire trace with crimped loops at either end. One loop takes a quick-release rig, holding the popper and the other is pushed into a sliding crimp sleeve on the main trace. First job is to thread the popper trace through the deadbait using a baiting needle. Then the popper is attached and the trebles nicked in place on the bait. Andy prefers the popper in the body cavity so it fishes tail down, or on the mouth of a whole bait. The other loop on the popper trace is pushed into the sliding crimp sleeve on the main trace. Adjust so the popper is hard against the bait.

a deadbait stick into the cavity of the bait, or use a coloured bait popper on a separate link, passing it through the bait so it sits directly above it. I'm sure a bright red popper enhances the presentation.

By using poppers, and adjusting buoyancy by using more or fewer of them, the bait can be fished directly above the lead or very slow sinking for a soft touchdown, as well as suspended just off the bottom. A couple of quick-change, pop-up weights enable you to adjust the height.

In coloured water, I carefully inject concentrated flavour into the flesh of the deadbait with a syringe. I've had a lot of success using fruit flavours mixed with oil, strawberry and tuna oil being one of the most successful.

RODS FOR DIFFERENT METHODS

One rod covers all my pike fishing on rivers and lakes with live and deadbaits. A 12ft, 2.75lb test curve Predator SX has served me well for many years. It has sufficient backbone to launch a big bait at long range and set hooks at extreme distance using a drifter float. Although it has got plenty of power, it is not a brute and handles fish under the rod tip in the margins of lakes or rivers.

A 1000 size fixed-spool reel with a free-spool facility is the natural choice. I have a couple of spools for each reel – one loaded with 12 or 15lb fluorocarbon and the other with 20 or 30lb floating braid.

For boat fishing, I prefer a shorter rod, not only in the overall length but also the size of the handle. There is limited room afloat so a shorter butt is an advantage. A 10ft boat rod is proficient at handling a big pike at close quarters when you are extremely low to the water. Exactly the same reel can be used as for fishing from the bank.

Lure fishing with jerk baits requires a short rod of 6ft 6in. The tip must be swiftly jerked downwards to impart action into the lure, so the rod needs to be much stiffer than for other methods. If the tip bends on the retrieve, you will lose action in the lure.

A jerk bait tends to glide up alongside the main line and tangles easily unless you use a stiff, solid wire trace. A multiplier is the best choice of reel, with a good level wind for line control. Low-stretch braid of 30 or 40lb is a must to withstand the colossal stresses on the tackle.

EARLY WARNING BITE INDICATORS

For bank fishing, I use a Frontrunner-style rest with a deep groove for friction-free line flow at the front of the rod, and a Duo Grip rear rest to hold the butt in position securely. A bite indicator is of huge importance to get the earliest possible warning of a take and I use a drop-off style alarm. This has a large head with a friction-free line gate connected to an audible alarm. Once the rig has been cast out, I tighten the line and put it in the clip, which I pull up hard against the spool of the reel.

When stillwater pike fishing, I have an open bale arm. On rivers, I set the free spool so it only just gives line against the current. This sensible system will cope with full-blooded takes and delicate dropbacks. The head of the alarm has a mercury switch that triggers the electronics once it drops below the horizontal. If you get a fast, straight take, the line falls from the clip, allowing the head to drop and trigger the alarm. This set-up can be used with legered bait, paternoster rigs and even as back-up when fishing deadbaits under a pencil float.

The Fox Micron drop-off bite alarm instantly alerts you to runs and dropbacks. It can be used with an open bale arm or baitrunner. The head lights up and the alarm sounds when the tilt action sensing system is triggered. Line is clipped in a polished gate pin on the head, which is hung directly below the reel spool.

River systems, large stillwaters and venues such as the Norfolk Broads, are more effectively fished from a boat than the bank. As well as all the essential safety gear, you need specialist boat rests and an electronic echo sounder for plotting underwater features and locating large shoals of bait fish. The latest sounders will log the co-ordinates of successful hotspots. A 15ft dinghy is big enough for two anglers to fish comfortably, and a boat of this size is easily transported by trailer and launched from public slipways. You need to check registration and licensing on most waterways.

Another type of boat that is winning favour for pike fishing is the bait boat. One of these makes it possible to fish well beyond normal casting range, and to drop bait accurately in potential hotspots. Top of the range models include echo sounders and GPS.

Acrobatic pike jettisons Andy's deadbait in the Mole Relief Channel.

RIGHT: Dusk is the magic hour in barbel fishing. This 12lb 6oz barbel rattled the rod tip in fading light on the Hampshire Avon's Royalty fishery at Christchurch.

BELOW: Fluorocarbon sinks like a stone and is almost invisible in water. Just what you need for catching spooky barbel.

4 Barbel

THE HARD-FIGHTING BARBEL, A FISH has become a cult species over the last decade, due to its huge increase in size and its successful colonisation of waters nationwide. Ten years ago, you wouldn't have risked a bet on the British record exceeding 20lb, but the Great Ouse has defied the odds. Double-figure fish are now the specimen standard and they're catchable on more than 20 rivers. Barbel over 15lb are regularly reported and four rivers have produced fish topping 18lb.

Quality baits have clearly boosted barbel weights, and the fish's torpedo shape and ability to hug the bottom in the strongest currents enable it to tolerate a changing environment. Vast reductions of permeable land on

floodplains have led to faster run-offs and river velocities. These conditions push out more fragile species during savage winter floods and barbel populations benefit. Today's barbel angler thinks nothing of using an 8oz lead to grip the bottom in winter floods.

Barbel flourish in a variety of river conditions, from the upper reaches down to murky tidal waters. They feed all year, providing the water temperature remains above 42°F. Occasionally, they are caught at lower temperatures but this is the exception. Once the river warms to 45°F they are a reliable fish to target.

Barbel are capable of living to a ripe old age, beyond 20 years. On most rivers, they spawn towards the end of May and often into June. They are

Stalemate on the Berkshire Loddon. When barbel dive into thick cover it's often best to give slack line and wait for them to emerge.

relatively slow growing in their early years and it's rare to catch them until they weigh over a pound. Experts predict that barbel scaling over 25lb will emerge within 20 years.

Although barbel are regarded as a species of fast-flowing rivers, some fishery owners have controversially stocked them in lakes. They appear to do well, displaying exceptional growth rates. Fears that high water temperatures in summer would cause problems appear to have faded, although they do not spawn. It's possible they will evolve to breed in time. My experience of lake barbel is that they fight well, and I'm not a critic of their appearance in small stillwaters. At least it gives us an extra lake species to tackle, especially in winter.

BAITS FOR EARLY SEASON

Barbel are generally found in fast, gravel glides flanked by weed-beds. Fishing for them in early summer is often tough because, after spawning, they gather in shallow, fast-flowing areas to forage on natural larders in order to regain peak condition. Small baits – particles, maggots and casters – are the ones to use. Small halibut pellets also produce bites.

Throughout the summer months, barbel continue to seek the swiftest of currents and, in clear water, they can set your pulse racing as they ghost across the gravelly bottom. On powerful rivers, turbulent water below weir-sills is another great barbel haunt.

By day, they shun open swims that lack cover, and tuck under the bank below overhanging trees and bushes, moving out at dusk to feed on clean, open gravels. Sometimes they venture into water barely deeper than their bodies.

In swims they are known to frequent, barbel respond to careful pre-baiting with a baitdropper. Ideally, feed several spots and watch how the fish behave over the tightly grouped beds of bait. Bide your time until they start feeding aggressively, losing their natural caution. It's possible to extract a whole shoal of barbel by adopting a stealthy approach.

Early season baits include plenty of hempseed, which barbel find irresistible. Six baitdropper helpings are sufficient to excite the fish for several hours. Hemp is easily digested and quickly passes through the system, unlike boilies, halibut pellets or other highly nutritional baits. Feed too many of these into the swim and the barbel quickly become overfed and drift away to digest their meal slowly.

Maggots used to be the top bait in summer and are still used to catch barbel on many rivers. But, small halibut pellets have become more popular, probably because they are more convenient than maggots, which need careful preparation and storage.

The barbel has become a much admired cult species. Dean Derbyshire of Poole pursues them on his local Dorset Stour and watched this 11-pounder snatch a pellet almost at his feet.

AUTUMN PREDICTABILITY

September is the start of the barbel season proper. The fish feed for longer periods as the days shorten and particle baits should be replaced by larger offerings. Barbel move into deeper glides where spotting them isn't quite so easy, but study the water and you'll still notice a distinctive flash as they grub around on the gravel, partly rotating on to their sides to reveal a fleeting glimpse of their flanks. The barbel's orange fins can be picked out on deeper gravel runs, and they porpoise on the surface at dawn and dusk.

Barbel are often regarded as exclusively bottom feeders, but there are times when they feed well off the bottom. They even suck food from the underside of

Praying for a pull at dawn above Schoolbridge at Throop fisheries on the Dorset Stour.

Halibut pellets in various diameters up toa size of 14mm are widely used as feed and hookbaits in UK barbel rivers.

weed, which is a spectacle I've witnessed many times. I once caught three surface-feeding barbel on floating crust in the Royalty's Parlour Pool at Christchurch in Hampshire.

Feeding a steady stream of maggots will persuade barbel to rise in the water and snatch them at mid-depth, but they are more difficult to hook when they feed like this – a good reason for introducing your bait on the bottom rather than throwing it in by hand and letting it slowly sink through the swim.

Providing the weather remains reasonably mild, barbel are at their most predictable in the autumn. It's bonanza time when autumn rains flush the dying weed from the river. You'll catch barbel throughout the day and night when rivers run slightly higher than summer level with a tinge of colour.

At this time of the year, I switch to bigger, smelly baits. For static fishing, larger halibut pellets and boilies are my first choice. This method is economical because you need just a handful of bait to attract fish into the swim. The pulling power of quality pellets and boilies is amazing. In late autumn and winter, six of these introduced close to the hook bait in a small PVA bag or stringer soon attract barbel to investigate your bait. Action comes very quickly and I rarely give a hotspot more than a couple of hours before trying the next one.

In pressured venues and known hotspots that are regularly fished, it's sometimes necessary to stay on after dark to catch fish. I've also had success on heavily fished waters by arriving at first light. In the past, barbel were viewed as late feeders and it wasn't worth starting until after lunch, but I believe their habits change when they are under constant pressure. The great thing about early morning sessions is that you often have the river to yourself and the pick of the swims.

ROVING WITH ROLLED MEAT

Autumn and winter are a great time for roving with rolled meat, which has never lost its effectiveness. The method involves trundling a big chunk of meat through the swim in a natural manner, slightly slower than the speed of the current. Barbel forage on food scraps washed down by the current, and glide several yards across the river to intercept something they've scented. This is the most productive method of all because each swim is quickly and comprehensively covered and you rove a lot of river in the day.

Winter floods may look unfishable but barbel are still easily caught if you bear in mind that they will be pushed from their regular haunts by the extra water. Heavily stained water actually improves your chances, providing there isn't too much debris in the river. They much prefer a strong, steady current over a clean bottom and will avoid swirling eddies where debris builds up. Specialist tackle is needed to cope with powerful currents. During floods, I spice up my boilies, luncheon-meat and paste baits with extra flavour. Added spicy and savoury smells ensure that the barbel quickly find your bait, even in a raging torrent.

When the weather is freezing and water temperatures really start to drop, I don't think barbel are worth targeting. I believe they find a comfortable spot on the riverbed and enter a state of semi-hibernation. I've seen a shoal of barbel apparently sleeping on a backwater of the River Kennet. From memory, the water temperature was about 40°F and the barbel were covered from head to tail by fine silt washed down in the flood. I gave one fish a prod with my landing-net pole, believing it might be sick, but it woke up and the shoal fled!

PELLETS WITH A LOLLIPOP

Most of my barbel fishing revolves around legering, but the float shouldn't be ignored. The late Jack Harrigan used to take enormous bags of barbel by trotting a quill and cork float, using a centrepin reel. The method was so deadly that it provoked a maggot ban on the Royalty for several years.

I think float fishing with pellets would prove equally deadly in the right swims. An example is one with deep margins and a gravel bed, where a 17ft rod and centrepin reel can be fished with a lollipop float a few feet downstream of the rod tip. Lollipop floats allow the rig to be held back in fast currents with the bait presented over-depth. A large olivette weight is used, resting against a small swivel that joins a lower-strength hook link to the rig. A couple of smaller dropper shots ensure the bait is fished tight on the bottom. This is a very precise, delicate way of presenting bait at close-quarters.

Long trotting with a larger Loafer or Avon float is another possibility, especially where the bait can be run down under overhanging trees and bushes

Andy fights his way through a willow tree to follow a big Wey barbel hooked on light gear.

that are difficult to probe with a standard leger. A heavy-duty float rod and free-running centrepin control the rig well. Donning a pair of chest waders and neckbag of bait and taking to the water is a superb way of tackling barbel in awkward swims.

TACKLE CHOICE

Major advances in barbel tackle have taken place over the last few years. Multi-top leger rods are very versatile and one model meets most demands. My choice is a rod supplied with swappable tops of 1lb 8oz and 1lb 12oz test curve, plus a quivertip section with several interchangeable tips. For downstream fishing, I use the solid standard top of 1lb 8oz, and reach for the heavier 1lb 12oz section when the river runs faster. Quivertips come into their own when upstream fishing – they show up dropbacks more readily and are less likely to dislodge the rig than a solid standard top. At night, I fit a sight tip to the top of the rod into which a chemical starlight capsule is inserted.

In heavy floodwater, I use a specialist barbel rod with a 2lb 12oz test curve that's capable of casting jumbo feeders and large leads. Another of my barbel rods is a three-piece, 15ft model, which was developed for big, wide tidal rivers, such as the Trent, where you need leads of up to 8oz. I prop the rod high so that as much line as possible is kept out of the water, and to stop the rig being dragged out of position.

Reel lines obviously vary from swim to swim and I carry spools of 6, 8, 10 and 12lb. I'm not a great fan of braid for barbel fishing, and fish exclusively with fluorocarbon, straight through to the hook. This line has proved revolutionary and might have been purpose-designed for barbel. It has less stretch than standard mono but still provides a slight buffer compared with unforgiving braid. It sinks quickly and its invisibility underwater is a great advantage in summer. Fluorocarbon's abrasion-resistant qualities mean it will absorb punishment in weed and over gravel. Finally, it has got fantastic knot strength and suits my rigs.

I use a 7000 size fixed-spool reel with a good front clutch, and a free spool, which is useful when fishing multiple rods. I like a quality centrepin for casting close to the bank because it maintains the right degree of tension on the rig. It also retrieves line under maximum pressure and provides audible indication through the ratchet when a barbel tears off with the bait.

BELOW LEFT: Barbel bites are violent and single rod rests provide more security than pods. A tight fitting rear rest also helps to boost stability.

A specialist landing net is vital – you often need to push it through weed in strong currents. I prefer a teardrop shape with free-flow mesh and a strong aluminium frame. A long, telescopic handle is also useful on high banks. Beware 'put-in' handles – I've seen them detach as a big fish is being pulled back against the current.

A solid rod rest for static fishing is important in a barbel set-up. Two separate bank sticks are preferable, so the rod isn't ripped from the rests by a violent take. A deep grooved front rest allows line free passage with a centrepin or free-spool reel. The rear grip must hold the handle tightly for security.

BELOW: **A sea-going barge ploughs through barbel swims on the tidal Trent below Cromwell Weir.**

USING A BAITDROPPER

Mobility matters in barbel fishing, so reduce the gear to a minimum. Pack a lightweight quiver with rods, rests and landing-net handle, and carry a bait bucket and light, low chair for comfort. Use a small shoulder bag for the rest and expect to switch swims, even when static legering.

In clear water, prime several swims with a few handfuls of bait and fish them in rotation. A baitdropper is a must for accurately placing the bait. Since a dropper never casts quite as well when attached to a rig, I prefer to use a separate rod and tie the dropper permanently to the end of 10lb line. With practise, you can introduce bait into far-bank swims, placing it just where you want it. Dull-coloured droppers eliminate bright flashes underwater when the trapdoor opens. I camouflage old brass models with a felt-tipped pen.

A mix of casters, hemp and pellets will interest a shoal of barbel for hours. Introduce between six and a dozen dropper loads into several swims at the beginning of a session, and allow plenty of time for the barbel to become preoccupied. Barbel are greedy feeders, which makes them easy to catch. Once a hook penetrates the underslung, rubbery mouth, it rarely pulls free. Fishing downstream, you'll need to hang on to the rod when a barbel bites. Immediately it feels resistance, the fish bolts downstream, jolting the rod tip and usually hooking itself. Self-hooking is guaranteed with a large semi-fixed lead and hair-rigged bait.

HOOKS, HAIR-RIGS AND FLEXI-RING SWIVELS

I used to think that short hook links were necessary for barbel, but these days I rarely use anything less than 12in. between hook and leger weight. I tie up a fluorocarbon trace and hook to match the size of bait. For example, a size 10

Create a dinner-table of feed on clean gravel using a baitdropper. This versatile Fox design offers interchangeable base weights and extension stems.

suits a 14mm boilie or pellet while a size 14 teams with hair-rigged casters or mini pellets. I recommend strong, eyed patterns with a slightly in-turned point. Eyed hooks make it easy to tie a 'knotless knot' hair-rig and in-turned points are less likely to be damaged on gravel.

Choice of leger weight is an in-line flat pear or Kling-on. I always use a flexi-ring swivel between main line and hook link, and wedge it into the safety sleeve of the leger so that it's semi-fixed and the hook link is attached to the ring, which automatically folds back out of harm's way during the cast. This is important to protect the hook-link knot from damage when the rig hits bottom.

In some swims, especially during the summer, it's advisable to position an additional back-lead a couple of feet from the leger weight to pin the main line to the bottom, where it is less likely to be detected by barbel.

If I'm hair-rigging casters, I put an artificial on the hair and superglue three natural casters around it. Hard halibut pellets need drilling out to hang on the hair and are held in place with a pellet stop that wedges into the drilled hole. Standard boilie stops are not effective because they are easily dislodged by small fish, and this allows the pellet to fall off.

Hair-rigged luncheon meat is a key method in winter floods. Heavily spiced, big chunks of meat are mounted on a specialist meat hair-rig system that ensures the hair doesn't tear through the side of the bait.

ABOVE: **Semi-fixed pellet presentation. A flexi-ring swivel lets the hook link fold back on the cast, preventing damage when it hits the gravel bottom.**

RIGHT: **Once a hook penetrates the barbel's gristly mouth it rarely falls out.**

FEEDER CHOICES AND PVA BAGS

Feeders play a big role in barbel fishing and I chiefly use block-ends or large open-enders. An in-line block-end is perfect for maggot and caster fishing, but the feeder must be heavy enough to anchor in place, otherwise you'll distribute bait across the swim instead of one tight area. Maggots soon exit a blockend feeder and the speed of discharge often needs slowing by blanking holes with electrical tape. The alternative is a Fox Freeflow block-end. This has a rotary body on which the discharge rate is adjusted by closing down the size of the holes. Casters and hemp wash from a block-end at a steady rate and it's worth making between 10 and 20 casts with the feeder alone to bait up the swim before attaching the hook bait.

A large open-end feeder comes into its own on big rivers, such as the Severn, Trent and Thames. Again, these are fished semi-fixed with the addition of a rig stop and bead above the swivel of the feeder and a bead and stop swivel below. This feeder is superb for carrying pellets and boilies into powerful, deep swims. The freebies are trapped between plugs of groundbait, which dissolve on the bottom allowing the offerings to tumble free.

Some swims are so powerful that you need to attach extra weight to hold station. I've got models carrying up to 10oz of lead, which I've glued on with Araldite. Long hook links are usually essential in these powerful swims as freebies released from the feeder might not settle on the bottom for a couple of feeds. I've used hooks links as long as 4ft in these circumstances.

Powerful tidal waters, like the Trent at Collingham, demand jumbo-sized barbel feeders. Andy modified his open-enders by attaching extra weights using Araldite. Fresh boilies go down well with Trent barbel, despite the heavy use of pellets.

PVA bags are another excellent way of accurately introducing tight beds of bait. I prefer tubular, woven mesh to solid bags. These work well with pellets. In summer and autumn, I frequently use three different sizes of pellets as barbel become more preoccupied with these than a single size. In winter I use a smaller bag because four to six larger pellets are all that are required.

All these methods rely on accurate baiting – precise casting delivers more efficient baiting and therefore more fish.

ROLLING MEAT

This is a magical method of catching barbel – and a stunningly simple concept. The clever bit is fine tuning the rig and sensing when the bait is being nosed by a fish. All you need do is attach a hook to the end of your main line and add sufficient weight just above it to allow the bait to work through the swim tight to the bottom.

The amount of extra weight added above the bait depends on current speed and type of swim. I try to get the bait trundling through without constantly snagging, or rolling so quickly that it doesn't momentarily hold back from time to time. That's why the weighting needs fine tuning until you get it exactly right.

Many anglers advocate using Plasticine but I prefer non-toxic shot in 1, 2 and 3 SSG sizes. In winter, it's not unusual to use the equivalent of 8 SSG to get the bait rolling effectively, but that's when conditions are at their best.

Ideally, the shot should be placed 4in. from the bait, but in very clear conditions 12in. might be better. If the weight is too close, it can sometimes spook the barbel. I find that the hardness of split-shot transmits a better feeling of bottom contact over gravel, which in turn paints a much better picture of what is below the surface.

This approach is exclusively for big chunks of meat, or the soft paste equivalent of a 1in. cube. It is no method for hair-rigs because they could easily snag in weed or debris. The bait is mounted directly on the hook, ideally a wide-gaped size 4 or even 2. Weighting the hook itself helps ensure the bait is fished as close to the bottom as possible. Some anglers wrap lead wire or putty around the shank of the hook to pin the bait down. My method is to leave a long tail on the hook knot, firmly pinch a swanshot on to it and then press the shot back into the bait.

Many specialists advocate braided lines for trundling meat, but I get fantastic feedback from fluorocarbon as the bait rolls through the swim, and it provides better presentation by sinking instantly.

Rolling meat allows you to search a huge amount of water quickly, exploring all the spots where barbel are likely to be lying. Wherever possible, I cast at an angle between 10 and 2 o'clock, which provides better bite detection and contact with the bait. Once you have cast out, take up most of the slack but leave a small bow in the line and keep adjusting this as the bait rolls downstream. Hold the line between thumb and forefinger to feel for bites, and twitch the bait to keep it on the move. Studying the bow of line between rod tip and water surface, and feeling the vibrations transmitted up the fluorocarbon line over your fingers, is surprisingly revealing once you've mastered the art. You develop a keen sense of how the bait is working and anything that doesn't feel quite natural could be a bite. These vary depending on how the barbel are feeding and where your bait is located relative to where you are standing. When you are fishing slightly upstream, a bite may be indicated by slack line. At other times, the bait might stop dead in its tracks. Once the bait moves downstream, the rod tip just wrenches around. I strike at anything that feels suspicious!

Explore all the usual gravel runs and glides, run the bait below overhanging bushes and try rolling between thick weed-beds. Rolling meat is one of the most underrated barbel methods, especially in this era of pellets and boilies.

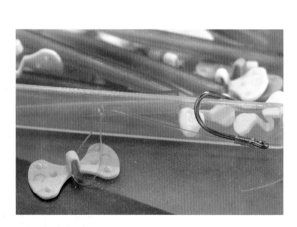

Ordinary stops easily pull through hair-rigged soft meat. But the Fox stop and sleeve system spreads the load and keeps the meat intact.

The sleeve and stop prevents the hair ripping out on a hard cast. Slide the meat on the hair using a closed-lip baiting needle. Then push the tapered sleeve onto the baiting needle, so the tapered end penetrates the meat first. Catch the needle in the hair loop, pull the sleeve inside the meat and wedge the stop in place.

Low tide on the tidal Trent and another strong specimen puts a serious bend in the rod.

A VITAL BREATHER

Barbel are extremely hard fighting and expend all their energy during a lengthy battle. They are usually dramatically weakened once they reach the net and require a resting period to recover their strength. It is imperative to hold them upright facing the flow in a steady current. Release a barbel prematurely and it could become wedged in weed-beds downstream and drown. It's not unusual for a barbel to take as long as ten minutes to recover. Wait until you feel the fish fighting against your grip before releasing it in an open, steady swim where it is easily observed gliding into the current. It's a satisfying sight to watch a big barbel swim powerfully away and take up its position on the gravels again. Little wonder they have become such a cult species.

Trent barbel from the turbulent tidal reaches below Collingham, where populations have boomed despite heavy cormorant predation.

RIGHT: Andy's personal best tench of 12lb 9oz hooked on boilies from Wintons fishery at Burgess Hill. During the same session he landed a male fish of 10lb 1oz to make it a notable double. (Photo: Greg Meenehan/ *Angler's Mail*)

BELOW: The wire thickness, profile and strength of a Super Specialist hook make it a safe choice for battling tench.

5 Tench

TENCH ARE FISH OF HIGH SUMMER, traditionally associated with lily-choked swims on old estate lakes shrouded in early morning mist. But modern tench fishing has mainly been transferred to massive gravel pits and reservoirs. Smaller lakes and ponds still produce bags of medium-sized fish, but most hefty specimens dwell in larger, clearer waters, where thick weed growth promotes rich, natural food larders.

Tench were nicknamed 'doctor fish' because of their fabled healing powers. According to myth, tench mucus was capable of clearing up wounds on fish that rubbed against them. That is obviously fanciful, but one unique fact about tench is that it's possible to sex them externally – the male's large, scallop-shaped pelvic or ventral fins are often three times larger than the female's. It may be that the extra large fins have evolved to help the male fan milt over the female's eggs.

Females carry up to 200,000 eggs, which dramatically increases their weight before spawning, which occurs from April to July, depending on water temperature. A ripe female can scale an extra 4lb above normal maximum weight. Unlike other species, maximum weights appear to have peaked in the UK – the number of double-figure fish caught today is the same as ten years ago – and the record is threatened only by the capture of females carrying abnormal quantities of eggs.

These fish are slow growing and long lived – veterans of 20 years are not unusual. I'd define a specimen tench as a fish over 8lb. A 10-pounder qualifies as the fish of a lifetime, while a 12lb tench is the ultimate prize for most specialists.

It used to be thought that male fish were substantially smaller, but double-figure specimens are taken every season, and there's speculation that genetic changes might have occurred. Males also seem to fight a lot harder than females, possibly due to their bigger fins. A 5lb male tench usually gives a far better account of itself than an 8 or 9lb female.

Tench have some of the smallest scales of any freshwater fish, making them very smooth to the touch, and almost eel-like. Their tiny, teddy bear, red eyes and rounded fins give them a chubby appearance. Colouration is largely influenced by habitat, and ranges from pale green through to near black. Subspecies of golden and yellow tench are bred for the ornamental trade. In clear gravel pits, tench are a classic olive green with a yellow to orange hue on the belly.

Frensham Great Pond has got a reputation for growing tench of high average size, like this 7lb 5oz stunner.

SPECIALISED DIET

Although tench are very widespread in rivers, lakes and canals, the best fishing is usually confined to large, clear gravel pits and reservoirs. They are mostly targeted between April and September and more spawn-bound fish have been captured since the introduction of all-year-round fishing on stillwaters.

I'm surprised that tench haven't capitalised to a greater extent on the pellets and boilies thrown into lakes. Specialists expected fish of 20lb to emerge, but it hasn't happened. I think the tench's specialised diet is the reason. They are happy to pick up boilies and pellets but spend much of their time grazing on tiny pea snails in heavy weed. Clearly, these molluscs do not have the same nutritional value as anglers' baits.

For tench, there is no better hook bait than casters, or a combination of casters and hemp, which reflects their natural food preferences. Mini boilies and small pellets are always a good alternative, with other natural baits such as worms, maggots and even big pieces of flake worthy of consideration. Many authors recommend freshwater mussels but I haven't seen any evidence to suggest that tench spend much time digging out juvenile swan mussels. They work quite well but appear to require a fair amount of pre-baiting.

Tench like to dig for bloodworm in silt pockets, so where these pockets occur there's a strong case for using red maggots, brandlings or small redworms, all of which are very useful for stalking large tench.

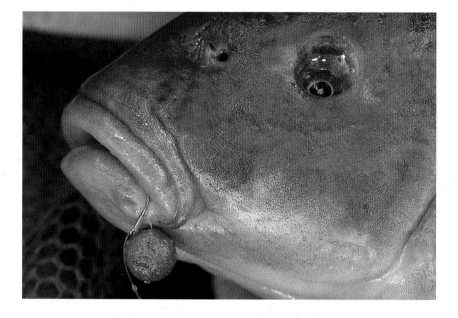

LEFT: **Tench in carp lakes tend to follow local flavour trends, but usually prefer a fresh soft boilie.**

Paddle-tailed male tench put up a deceptively furious fight.

FINDING FISH

Tench are nomadic fish and follow a favourable wind to where plenty of oxygen and a warming thermocline concentrate natural larders in a small area. They often roll before diving with a splashy tail movement. On calm days, they send up patches of tiny bubbles that are easily tracked through the swim.

Tench tend to patrol underwater features – bars, plateaux and islands, especially those with steep, shelving sides and rapid changes in depth. They are chiefly bottom feeders but spend a lot of time swimming aimlessly in mid-water. Stand on the side of a clear gravel pit and you can watch small groups of tench cruising up and down all day.

Where no visual signs of tench are on show, I rely on wind direction to give me a clue. Tench are one of the few fish to respond in the teeth of a gale, provided it's a warm wind. They relish days when large waves crash into the margins, discolouring the water for many yards back out into a clear lake. Look closely between the waves and you'll often spot splashy tench rolls.

Tench were once regarded as highly nocturnal but in most waters they are far easier to catch in daylight. The only conditions they don't like are flat calm and still days.

Weed and tench go together. These fish are great at digging out food items trapped in weed, and raking out a swim is time well spent, but do it in a limited area only. If you create too large a gap in a bed of weed, the tench will give it a miss. Traditional weed rakes flung out on the end of a rope form clear channels in the weed and, in my experience, tench treat these clearings as no-go zones. I prefer to make round holes, 2–3ft in diameter, using a weed-cutter screwed into the end of a long-handled landing-net pole. Once cleared, regular baiting will keep it that way as tench root out freebies. Small spots such as these should produce consistent action for several weeks before the tench become suspicious.

SUBSTANTIAL GEAR

Tench are more rig shy than most species in still waters. They have a frustrating ability to clear up all the freebies and leave the hook bait. When I'm using scaled-down carp rigs with hair-rigs and boilies, I'm convinced that tench pick up the bait dozens of times before being hooked. These rigs must be fine tuned to succeed.

Tench are powerful fighters and you need substantial gear to extract them from weedy swims. Line strengths of 6–10lb are my choice, depending on weed density, dropping to between 4 and 8lb in open water. A 13ft float rod with a tippy action and powerful middle and butt section is just the job for punching out big wagglers, as well as a more delicate straight peacock float for the lift method.

For leger and feeder fishing, a 12ft barbel-style rod with a test curve of 1lb 8oz provides plenty of backbone for chucking out weighty feeders and controlling a big tench in thick weed. A 7000 size reel with a free-spool facility is an added bonus. For feeder and leger fishing, multiple rods are often used with buzzers and light bobbins.

For most of my tench fishing I use fluorocarbon line, which has the right characteristics for extracting big tench from weed. Hooks must be strong and Super Specialists are my first choice eyed hooks for hair-rigs. I use a spade-end for hook-mounted baits and recommend Super Spades.

A flat calm at the dam end of Hollowell Reservoir, belies the drama unfolding below Andy's rod tip as large tench tear up the bottom weed to get at his casters.

LIFT METHOD

For close range, just beyond the near shelf, I use a waggler and fish the lift method. Providing not too many nuisance fish are in the vicinity, which is unlikely in open pits, a 50–50 mix of casters and hemp is my first line of attack. These are catapulted to concentrate the bait within a 1-yard circle. A straight peacock is attached bottom end only and held in place with a couple of rubber float stops. The bulk of the weight is fixed 18in. above the hook with a tell-tale No. 1 shot 2in. away. The float is shotted down until only a tiny part of the sight tip is left showing.

Having carefully plumbed the swim, I ensure the tell-tale shot just kisses the bottom. I use 4lb fluorocarbon line straight through from reel to hook, and mount a couple of casters on a size 16 Super Spade. To get the float in the right position, I over-cast the swim, sink the line and gradually retrieve the rig into position. It's wise to put the rod on a couple of rests with the rod tip positioned just below the surface to prevent wind causing false bites. Every bite should induce the float to rise in the water by an inch as the No.1 shot is lifted by the taking tench. This gives the earliest indication of any take and helps outsmart finicky feeders.

Lift float rig.

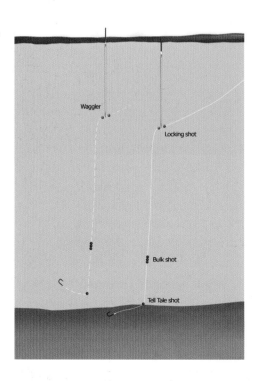

Waggler

Locking shot

Bulk shot

Tell Tale shot

Tench weights fluctuate down the seasons in Frensham Great Pond but their beautiful olive colourations and classic shape remain constant.

SLIDER SYSTEM

I switch to large sliders for deeper water farther out, and prefer models with base weights that carry about half the total load for the float. You need at least 6lb line to cast these big sliders any distance and I fix an additional tiny swivel just below the bulk shot, which could be up to 6 SSG. A small, soft-rubber bead positioned just above this swivel protects the knot. I attach a lighter 12in. hook link to the swivel, and space two No. 6 shot along its length to provide stability when fishing fractionally over-depth. You may need to increase the size of these dropper shot on a windy day when there is a strong undertow.

To ensure the slider works efficiently, place a No. 1 shot 4ft from the hook, which prevents the slider dropping down on to the bulk shot. As well as allowing you to cast farther and more accurately, this arrangement encourages the float to slide up the line easily.

Most good sliders are equipped with tiny eyes and you just need to tie on a Billy Lane stop knot to set the depth. If you find the knot jams in the slider eye, place a small hard bead between the two.

For stability and sensitivity, I prefer hollow-tipped and vaned slider floats. Once the float is at the correct depth when cast into position, apply white Tippex on the line as a distance marker so you cast to the identical spot every

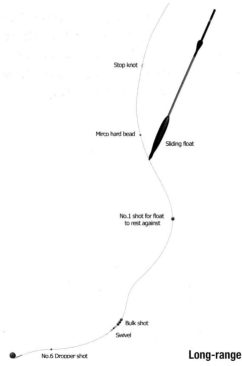

Stop knot

Mirco hard bead

Sliding float

No.1 shot for float
to rest against

Bulk shot

Swivel

No.6 Dropper shot

Long-range slider float rig.

time. For this type of fishing, I hair-rig mini boilies or small pellets of between 8 and 10mm. The float is a marker for accurate feeding of free offerings.

This set-up is also useful for presenting a maggot rig over soft, filamentous bottom weed. I feed dead red maggots – cleanly sieved before being frozen several days before the session – introducing them with a spod or rocket on a separate rod, again using the float as a marker. Two live red maggots are the hook bait, used with a buoyant artificial grub to give a soft touchdown over a weedy bottom. The reason for baiting with dead maggots is that they won't wriggle out of sight, and they hang naturally in the fronds of soft weed.

POLE RIG ON A LONG ROD

Swims with deep, clear margins are often best tackled with a long rod and pole rig. Where weed or snags are absent, I load 4lb line on a centrepin with a hi-tech hook link of the same breaking strain but much lower diameter. These are joined by a tiny size 20 swivel.

A 19 or 20ft float rod allows you to fish a pole float directly under the tip. This is one of the most accurate ways of fishing for tench and is devastating in the right conditions. A long-tipped pole float with a rugby ball shaped body is perfect. The bulk shot should be positioned just above the swivel and you can even use an in-line olivette instead of split shot.

The thinner hook link, between 9 and 12in. long, carries a couple of No. 8 dropper shots for good indication. I fish this rig at dead depth with a variety of baits including banded pellets, or specialist paste studied with tiny pellets, to fool a wise old tench. For deeper swims, a baitdropper is ideal for placing freebies straight on the bottom without attracting roach and rudd to free-falling baits.

A buoyant rubber grub on the shank and two natural reds on the bend, produces a slow sinking cocktail over weed.

You are more likely to get good returns in early season on Hollowell Reservoir, before the Canadian pondweed thickens up. This 7lb 9oz specimen was hooked in a clearing where bream were spawning.

FEEDER TACTICS

I guess feeder fishing is the most popular tench method and I normally adopt three lines of attack. The first of these features an in-line blockend with casters on the hook and a payload comprising a 50–50 mix of casters and hemp. After casting out and sinking the line, I give it a quick tweak by sharply moving 2in. of line towards me. This helps empty the feeder and pull my hook bait into the middle of the freebies. I usually tie a hook link of 6in. and fish the feeder semi-fixed, wedging the stop swivel into the central safety sleeve.

The next two set-ups both involve a Method mix groundbait. On a clear, gravel bottom I go for a standard Method feeder with three fins and centrally mounted weight. Over soft weed or on steep-sloping shelves, a flatbed feeder comes into its own. This ensures that the feeder always lands the same way up and gives it a high degree of stability.

For both feeders, I have a short hook link, between 3 and 6in. long, semi-fixed to the feeder itself. Baits are hair-rigged mini boilies or pellets, which are pressed back into the groundbait that is moulded around the feeder.

It's important that the groundbait mix is stiff and breaks down slowly. Specialist Method mixes, together with a few freebies and a helping of hemp, is a good starting point. Rather than using water to dampen down the mix, I prefer sticky corn steep liquor, which has great binding qualities and holds the mix intact until the tench start attacking it. Otherwise, it breaks down after 20 minutes.

In the right conditions, it is possible to create a feeding frenzy by regularly catapulting small balls of groundbait, similar in size to the feeder, into the swim. These create a large feeding table and usually draw in a substantial shoal of tench. The tench quickly wise up if you feed larger, tangerine-sized balls – they'll attack these and leave the smaller ones alone. Cast every 15 minutes – I'm convinced the tench get used to the noise of the groundbait hitting the surface of the water and are attracted to it. A take often comes within minutes of casting out but beware false bites caused by tench attacking the groundbait around the feeder. Ignore everything until you get a screaming run as the tench hooks itself on the very short hook link.

BAIT BOATS

Some lakes are like inland seas and tench feed well beyond casting range. A bait boat overcomes the problem. One of these is safer than trying to cast huge weights, which could crack off. I've seen barbaric, long-range rigs used to drag big tench from heavy weed. This crude approach with 5oz weights on heavy lines and braided hook links cannot be justified, no matter how successful.

A bait boat equipped with an echo sounder will soon map the bottom contours, as well as delivering a rig at very long range. Most bait boats deliver free offerings at the same time to provide the accurate groundbaiting that is necessary for successful tench fishing.

If fishmeal boilies fail on the Method feeder, bright Tutti Fruttis will sometimes switch on the tench to bite.

RIGHT: That's what you call a slab. It scaled 14lb 9oz and came from Harefield Lake in the Colne Valley.

BELOW: Quality ingredients ready for the mixing bowl on a carp lake where double-figure bream make short work of anything less substantial.

6 Bream

THERE ARE NO HALF MEASURES with bream – specimen hunters either admire or resent them. Bream are detested as slimy gatecrashers by carp anglers when a shoal wipes out their carefully constructed rigs in the dead of night, while other specialists treat them with respect – and you can include me in their fan club. A double-figure bream is a stunning looking creature, with a body that's the equivalent of a 20lb carp.

Bream grow slowly and survive for 20, or possibly 25, years. They are highly sociable. Fish of similar size and weight stay together in large shoals from egg to maturity, and monster bream appear to emerge from a particular season's spawning, or year-class. Maximum weights have soared almost off the graph in recent seasons and I'm confident a 20-pounder will eventually head the record-fish charts. Bream of this calibre have been found dead.

Many anglers believe high-quality baits are responsible for the huge weight gains, but some of the biggest bream survive on natural food larders that are found in vast, lightly fished waters. Trout reservoirs and gravel pits in the Colne Valley historically produce generations of monsters that have never seen a boilie or pellet. Climatic changes also influence bream growth, judging by how many double-figure bream are caught in the depths of winter. This was unknown until recently and is a good reason for rethinking the period for targeting bream.

This 11lb 6oz bream sneaked into a carp swim at Horseshoe Lake in the Cotswolds. It fought incredibly hard in the clear, weedy water.

GRAVEL PIT NOMADS

I start my bream sessions in May, before the breeding season, when I think they are at their most predictable. At this time, they feed aggressively in order to build up body fats in preparation for spawning. From early spring, males exhibit spawning tubercles over their nose, head and pectoral fins. These start as small bumps under the skin and are hardly visible. Nearer spawning, they turn white and grow to the size of matchstick heads. Males and females are of equal size but spawn-laden females can weigh a pound or two heavier.

Bream inhabit every type of water but gravel pits and reservoirs are prime venues. Tiny pits of just a couple of acres often support a handful of big bream and these fish certainly benefit from anglers' bait. Bream stocks in certain rivers are also showing a marked increase in weight. The odd double-figure fish now puts in an appearance in the middle reaches of the Thames.

I'd say double-figure bream are a relatively easy target in this new age of super specimens. I've increased my standard yardstick for a specimen to 12lb, and anglers who specialise in them will probably seek a 15-pounder. How targets have changed! Some anglers dismiss bream as fighting like a wet sack but, while they are certainly not the Mike Tysons of the specimen fish world, if you scale your gear down to a sensible level, these big slabs give a good account of themselves.

I've never found bream hugging the margins. They love wide, open spaces and often roam a fair distance from the bank. They don't like weed-beds or snags, preferring to circle around plateaux and patrol clean gravel bars where the depth varies by at least 2 or 3ft between peaks and troughs. Ideally, the drop-offs should be gently sloping rather than steep. Big bream are mostly at home in slightly deeper water – 10–15ft is ideal for them. They don't like to feed in shallow water or extremely deep swims.

Bream are notoriously nomadic, but find one and there should be plenty more of them. They cover huge distances, grazing the bottom for food, and usually feed at night in most waters. During the day, they often cruise close to the surface. You need to feed a big bed of bait to encourage a shoal of bream to stay in the swim, otherwise they'll quickly move on. They'll consume a couple of handfuls of bait in seconds.

Ski Lake at the London end of the M3 holds good shoals of nomadic bream, but there's no telling when they'll feed. The trigger is usually falling light levels.

FEEDING MASTERPLAN

Regular baiting educates bream into visiting the same spot night after night. You can almost set your watch by the first take of the evening and action is very predictable – it's like ringing the dinner bell. Regular baiting requires a lot of effort, though, especially as many of the best bream spots are up to 100 yards out from the bank, but time spent with a catapult and spod reaps benefits if you are prepared to put in the hours.

Bream capitalise on whatever food is available but the most consistent baits are pellets, boilies, maggots, worms and sweetcorn. Good-quality groundbaits, containing cereals and fishmeals, together with handfuls of hook baits must be fed in large quantities to keep a shoal of bream interested. In my experience, coarse groundbaits with large particles work better than finely sieved varieties. Bream are also attracted by boilie flavourings, and groundbaits can be given extra pulling power by including flavour within the mix. I try to discover the type of boilies and flavourings being used most regularly on a big-bream venue and include them as part of my groundbait mix. The groundbait should be of a very stiff consistency. A liquid binder, such as corn steep liquor, will hold the balls together so that they descend quickly without breaking up and then slowly disintegrate on the bottom.

Accurate baiting delivers better results than you might otherwise achieve. I use a marker float to pinpoint the target area and catapult or spod the groundbait tightly to it. A baited area 10ft in diameter allows quite a few fish to feed together, which plays on their competitive nature and ultimately brings more bites.

Bream will not tolerate groundbait crashing on their heads. If they come across a big baited area, they will stay there until every morsel has been eaten, but if you attempt another bombardment while they are still there, they'll

Forget traditional bream rigs on carp lakes holding large slabs. Buried in the stiff groundbait studded with mini boilies is a 28gr Fox Compact feeder. A 4in. hook link and size 14 barbel hook completes the set-up.

The relief shows as
Andy's 14lb bream
wallows into the net
on Harefield.

probably leave. They accept the odd feeder going in but not a barrage of tangerine-sized balls raining down.

This is why I bait up two or three separate areas, depending on how many rods I'm allowed to use. I keep the baited areas between 10 and 20 yards apart, ideally along the side of a gravel bar or edge of a plateau. Typically, the bream move in from one side and feed in that area before switching to the next spread of food. This gives you a chance to bait up the first hotspot again, but only when you are positive the bream have moved out.

If you are lucky enough to get it right, you can experience action throughout the night before the bream drift off at dawn. It's a case of getting yourself organised with plenty of groundbait, making sure you have spare elastics and pouches for your catapults and spod, and that rods and markers are at the ready. Bream fishing is hard work and time consuming but very exciting.

How much bait does it involve? I stagger along the bank with 10kg buckets of pre-mixed groundbait. I start off with 10 tangerine-sized balls in each hotspot and then, if all goes well, repeat it on a rota basis as the bream move in and out of the area.

To give you an idea of their appetites, on a couple of occasions I have pre-baited a swim with up to 5 kilos of groundbait, only for a big shoal of slabs to devour the lot in less than two hours. The critical thing is to put it in and leave it there to do its job without risking baiting up over the top. Sometimes the fish can move in within an hour, other times it may take several hours. Never risk scaring them off a baited area by being impatient.

BITE OR LINER?

For bream, I prefer to use barbel-type rods with test curves of 1lb 8oz or 1lb 12oz, and 7000 size reels loaded with 6lb fluorocarbon line, plus a 10 or 12lb shock leader of the same material if I'm banging out to the horizon. I set up the rods with buzzers and bobbins high above the ground so I can use a long drop on light indicators.

Big bream are renowned for giving spectacular line bites and you must sit on your hands and wait for the real thing. False bites might cause the bobbin to rise steadily towards the butt ring for a couple of feet before slowly dropping back. Striking at liners spooks the fish out of the swim.

I set the free spool so it gives line easily, even to a liner, and I don't strike until the bream is moving off steadily. All my rigs are self-hooking, so it's a simple case of picking up the rod and winding down until I feel the full weight of the fish before setting the hook.

These days, traditional bream rigs have been abandoned. Gone are the days

of long paternosters with 4 and 6ft tails. I don't know why we used them in the first place. When you think about it logically, the bream are attracted to a heavily baited area and compete for every morsel. We used to throw out a groundbait feeder with the hook bait 5ft away. What on earth were we thinking about? No wonder we had to endure liners for so long until the bream found our hook bait, miles away from the groundbait.

Buzzers and lightweight indicators give early warning of bream moving into the swim through line bites. Long drops are helpful to avoid striking at false takes.

All my rigs are based on short hook links of between 4 and 7in., and feeders are still my main line of attack – a three-finned Method-style feeder is my favourite. I mould stiff groundbait around the feeder and fish the hook bait hair-rig-style on a short hair. The inclusion of a flexi-ring swivel is a must to protect the hook-link knot from being damaged on the cast. Baits are usually 10mm

boilies, pellets or artificial corn. I've caught more big bream on rubber corn than on anything else in recent seasons. I prefer the buoyant variety and fish one or two grains on the hair with a counterbalance shot three-quarters of an inch from the hook. This usually nails the bream in the bottom lip and it is rare for one to fall off. The set-up is fished in-line and semi-fixed, so it is virtually a bolt rig.

Artificial corn is a brilliant way of combating the armies of signal crayfish that are on the march in many gravel pits. It's indestructible and eliminates the need to keep recasting with fresh hook bait. Softer baits are easily demolished by crayfish. I give artificial corn a boost by soaking the rubber kernels in bottles of boilie mix – the same flavour that I use in the groundbait mix.

Occasionally, I use open-end feeders when mounting maggots, worms or natural corn directly on the hook itself. I still use a very short hook link to keep the bait close to the feeder but I make the rig free-running, which allows me easily to monitor what is going on with the hook bait. You soon get to recognise the difference between a bite and a liner with this rig. Slow, long lifts of the bobbin that gently fall back again are liners. Real takes on a running rig are slightly sharper and jerky, sometimes moving the bobbin no more than a couple of inches.

The three styles of open-end feeder that I prefer suit varying types of bait and groundbait. In a cage feeder, I use an explosive mix, made up on the dry side with items such as crushed hemp that burst out once the water starts to penetrate.

Solid block-end feeders are useful for delivering larger freebies, such as a few grains of corn, boilies or pellet, sandwiched between plugs of stiffer groundbait. With the solid feeder, I normally cast out and leave it a couple of

BELOW LEFT: Fox Method feeder rig incorporating a size 14 hook, buoyant rubber corn and size 6 counterbalance shot.

BELOW: Finned groundbait feeders. The open-ender with oval holes takes heavier groundbait blends holding large particles like pellets. Solid feeders are plugged each end with groundbait to trap maggots or chopped worm in the middle. The cage model suits fluffy mixes.

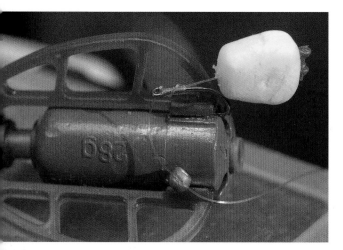

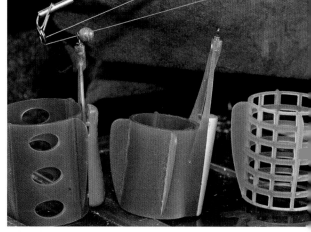

minutes before giving the rig a sharp twitch to release the contents and put the hook bait smack in the middle of the freebies.

The standard open-end feeder with holes is useful for mixing in livebaits, such as worms and maggots, among the groundbait. These eventually wriggle out and break down the rest of the contents.

SPOT-ON CASTS

To help maintain casting accuracy, tie a distance marker on the line. I use brightly coloured braid or electrical tape to ensure that my casts are spot on. Although big bream are caught on float gear, that doesn't suit the big open waters where I regularly target them. Bream follow the wind, provided it's a warm one, and this gives a good key to location. They show themselves at dusk and, with the aid of binoculars, you should be able to figure out which way they are moving and feed groundbait on their predicted path.

I've extended my bream sessions much later in the season. They can be caught regularly while the water temperature remains above 45°F.

Bream fishing generally means putting in night shifts, so you need to get organised by making up plenty of spare rigs. Pack replacement batteries for the head torch and position landing net, unhooking mat and weighing equipment so that you know exactly where they are in the pitch black. Dampen everything that's likely to make contact with the bream and return the fish as quickly as possible.

Plastic corn, along with other popped-up baits, usually produce a good hookhold in the scissors or bottom lip.

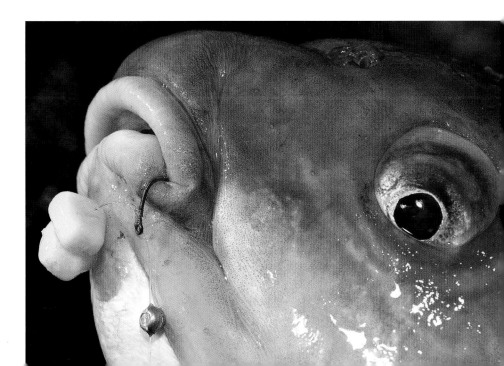

RIGHT: **Find golden gravels and a swift flow on rivers like the Dorset Stour and the dace shoals won't be far away.**

BELOW: **Shallow water float patterns for dace include the Puddle Chucker, which collapses on the strike.**

7 Dace

SHOALS OF FAST-BITING DACE have colonised the shallow, swift-flowing reaches of most UK rivers. They spawn towards the end of the traditional close season and congregate in huge numbers as they head towards their spawning grounds in side-streams and fast, gravel runs. They are slow growing and live for seven or eight years on most rivers, although they may occasionally reach 10 years old in the right conditions.

Dace, nicknamed 'silver darts', survived a worrying population crash in the 1990s when they practically disappeared from numerous rivers, including the Hampshire Avon. Many people blamed cormorant predation, but the species bounced back and stock levels have stabilised again.

Small chub are often mistaken for dace. The crucial difference is that the dace's fins are concave while the chub's are rounded. Also, the dace's mouth is much smaller and it is more silvery than a young chub.

Dace are obliging biters on bitterly cold days when nothing else feeds. Size for size, they fight as hard as any other species, especially in rapid water where they twist and turn to throw the hook.

The average size for a mature dace is 8 to 10oz and the species hasn't shown any increase in size in living memory. A 1lb dace is the specimen target for most specialists. Fish of this size can be caught across the country, but anything larger than 1lb is a rarity. In recent seasons, spawn-laden females have threatened the British record but only a handful of 1lb 4oz fish have ever been recorded.

CREATURES OF HABIT

The dace's behaviour patterns are unique. A long-term survey carried out by Dr Stuart Clough on the Dorset Frome, revealed an amazing daily migratory ritual. Several fish were radio tagged and tracked and the results showed that a shoal of dace spent most of the day in shallow, fast water, which they appeared to use as a safe resting area to evade predators. At night, they dropped downstream, sometimes by as much as two miles, to feed in deeper water before returning to exactly the same spot for their daily rest. Individual fish occupied an identical position each day within the shoal.

This research mirrors what I have seen with my own eyes as a shoal of dace

Matching specimen dace landed from London AA's Britford waters on the Salisbury Avon.

suddenly deserts a swim in the evening, leaving it devoid of life. Before Dr Clough's survey became available, I used to think that this behaviour was the result of an angler's presence on the bank, but it's clearly a long-established migration pattern.

On my own patch, dace shoals spawn on the same day every year in an identical spot on the river. This spectacle tends to occur around the middle of March, when thousands of dace move into an area where they are hardly seen for the rest of the year.

This behaviour goes a long way towards explaining why it is all or nothing with dace – you either bag up or blank. However, I have noticed that larger female fish often gather together in small groups and distance themselves from juvenile fish. Find these groups and you stand a chance of notching up a multiple catch of 1lb dace in a session. I've located pods of big females in the tiniest of backwaters, in water only a few inches deep. Time spent walking the river pays dividends if you are attempting to target larger specimens.

In fact, it is rare to find any mature dace mingling with juveniles, so I either go for the bigger fish, knowing I'm unlikely to catch more than six if I'm lucky, or for a big bag of smaller fish. It's great fun putting a 30lb net of 'darts' together when other species aren't feeding.

RIGHT: London AA bailiff Stuart Wilson has seen a dace explosion on the Hampshire Avon at Britford following years of decline. This session in a famous Harnham Island peg produced a 30lb net of dace and the same amount of chub.

LEFT: Net of small dace from the Dorset Frome at Wareham, where the species congregates in winter because of the warmer tidal waters.

STEADY FEEDING

Digital kitchen scales are essential to weigh a large dace accurately. Place the fish in a wire basket rather than damp weigh bag to eliminate errors. A 1lb dace is normally between 11 and 13in. long, depending on the river from which it was taken. Southern river specimens tend to be shorter and more pigeon-chested compared with their longer, thinner cousins in northern game rivers.

Dace prefer small food items, including fly larvae, pea snails and shrimps. Maggots, hemp and casters are the prime hook baits, interspersed with the occasional use of elderberries in autumn and tares in winter, when the fish may be a bit more selective.

Dace are willing feeders and a steady stream of bait gets them competing for every morsel. Little and often is the best feeding tempo. It's imperative that you introduce just sufficient to maintain the shoal's attention. Feed too much and the dace will start chasing bait downstream. This makes the difference between confident bites and ridiculously fast-feeding fish that are difficult to hook. Too many free offerings flowing through the swim split the shoal, encouraging them to chase around and leave much of the food untouched. A good indicator that you're feeding at the right level is when you attract a big shoal of dace under your rod tip.

Small shoals of big dace are a different matter. They can be deeply frustrating, initially refusing to accept free offerings. When this happens, I find that introducing the freebies in a baitdropper may get them eating. Food deposited with a baitdropper sticks closer to the bottom and trundles through the swim at a slower rate, which appears to be more attractive to bigger, older and wiser fish. They don't seem to be prepared to move station to intercept freebies, especially those that are coming through off bottom at the speed of the current.

There's barely enough water to cover the gravels in this River Wey swim at Farnham, but it's swarming with dace.

DIBBERS FOR FAST WATER

Just a couple of basic outfits are all that are required in dace swims. For float fishing, use a 13ft, tip-actioned match rod, designed for lines up to 4lb, teamed with a small fixed-spool or centrepin reel. An 11 or 12ft light feeder rod with soft, interchangeable quivers down to 0.8oz paired with the same fixed spool meets all other needs. It's rare for me to use reel lines over 2lb, but I favour low-diameter, hi-tech hook links of 0.08 and 0.10mm. These are joined to the main line by a tiny swivel, usually positioned directly below the float.

Small, stubby floats are the right choice for dace swims, which are typically no more than 9in. deep. For a top and bottom set-up, I've turned to small carp dibbers, which are bulbous with a large sight tip that is easily seen well downstream. In turbulent, shallow swims, a small Chubber float carrying up to a couple of swanshot is very useful while Avon floats are needed in swims over 18in. deep.

In clear water where shoals of dace are easily spooked, I fish a small Trent Trotter or Puddle Chucker bottom-end only. These make less disturbance on the strike than some other floats, because they fold back against the hook link when you leave a gap of 10mm between the locking shot. If you trap a waggler-style float between locking shot, leaving no room for movement, it will make a lot of noise and splash on the strike.

Dumpy pole floats perform well in the shallows. You'll achieve a smooth trot and see the float tip at range.

In floods, or when targeting larger fish, a small block-end feeder can produce results. Fish it free-running, stopped with a small swivel and couple of beads to protect the main line knot. Adjust the length of the hook link, which should be lighter and of a lower diameter than the main line, until you get positive bites. I start with a hook link of 18in. and then try a longer or shorter one, depending on how the dace are feeding.

In contrast to the bites you get with a float rig, you have to be more patient and let bites develop with a feeder set-up. I ignore little taps and pulls and strike only when there is a positive pull on the quiver.

Delicate dace prefer the well-oxygenated shallows near insect-rich weed fronds.

BARBLESS HOOKS

Hook choice is one of the key factors in dace fishing. Unlike for most other coarse fish, I recommend a barbless hook, because dace are not heavy enough to pull the point home beyond the barb. Their habit of twisting and turning in fast water makes it easy for them to spin free when the point has only just penetrated the skin. A barbless hook doesn't require weight to drive it home.

Hook sizes are 18 or 20 for single or double bait. Spade-end hooks are the norm, but I have recently experimented with eyed hooks. Several patterns are now available in the small sizes and fine wire that suit this style of fishing. Tying them up 'knotless knot' style, so that the hook link leaves on the inside of the eye, creates more of an acute angle that encourages the hook to stay in place.

Beaked or slightly in-turned points help in tying a spade-end hook so the link comes off the outside of the spade rather than the inside as normal. The aim is to create extra leverage and an angle so the hook remains in place. If I lose two or three fish, I immediately try something else. There are no set rules. Type of swim, float choice, depth and the way the dace are feeding dictates hooking success.

8 Crucian carp

That's a 4lb crucian rolling on top and Andy must proceed with caution on a 0.08mm hook trace. Scene of the action is Marsh Farm at Godalming, reputedly Britain's finest crucian water.

EVIDENCE OF THE INCREASED POPULARITY of crucian carp is that specialists have pinpointed a select number of venues where the species are known to be authentic. In the past, confusion over identification has led to many hybrids being claimed as record-breakers. A subspecies classified as a cross between a crucian and a common carp goes by the undignified name of brown goldfish.

This has all come about because of the ease with which king carp and crucians hybridise. In reality, if a venue contains both king carp and crucians, questions will always be raised over the authenticity of the crucian strain.

Hybrids can look similar to true crucians and it is difficult to be totally sure of identification using external examination alone. However, numerous pointers may help you to spot the real deal. Crucian carp have no barbels and are shorter and chubbier in appearance than common carp or hybrids, and they tend to have a browner overall colouration compared with king carp. Look closely at the fins for any hint of orange, as found on king carp. A crucian's fins are more rounded and have a softer feel than a king carp's, especially the dorsal and anal fins. The first ray isn't as hard or spiky. A lateral-line scale count is also a good guide to authenticity. There should be between 28 and 33 scales along the lateral line, from directly behind the gill cover to the root of the tail.

Crucians are widely distributed, but it is in the smaller, more intimate waters where they live on their own that the original genetic strain is likely to endure. Small estate lakes, ponds and test gravel workings are typical venues. Crucians don't seem to prosper in large gravel pits and they are not fans of moving water.

Growth rate is slow and there has been no marked increase in maximum weights. The only change in the British record has resulted from spawn-laden females being caught during the former close season. Crucians normally spawn during May, or possibly in early June, depending on the weather. A mature female of 4lb might carry 8 or 10oz of spawn if she is really ripe, but the average size of crucians is nearer 2lb. The target weight for the specialist angler is 3lb.

These fish are cantankerous feeders and if you are lucky enough to watch crucians feeding in clear water, you'll understand why. They move around slowly in tightly packed shoals, gently picking over the bottom in a painstakingly methodical manner, and are easily muscled out of the swim by tench, bream and even darting roach. Less appears to be known about their life cycle than about any other species. They naturally feed on tiny larvae, minute pea snails and juvenile shrimps, and they couldn't be described as ravenous feeders, which is probably a clue to their very slow growth rate.

It's thought that they live to a ripe old age, certainly 30 years, perhaps even longer. For me, this is what makes them such a fascinating species. They are the only fish that warrant being described as cuddly!

SUMMER TARGETS

Since the abolition of the old close season on stillwaters, the time for targeting crucians has been dramatically extended. For most of the winter, they appear to survive in a semi-torpid state and are rarely caught. They start moving in spring, once the water temperature begins to rise. I start fishing for them in April when, by crucian carp standards, they feed in earnest. I've had most of my best bags at this time and, providing the weather remains settled, they can be very predictable. The feeding spree carries on until the temperature rises sufficiently for them to spawn. They go off feed completely at spawning time, but once the ritual is over they get their heads down again.

Crucians do not spawn as aggressively as king carp, and so they recover more quickly and maintain better condition. They still look in tip-top shape, albeit a few ounces lighter, when caught immediately after spawning. Crucians remain active until the end of the summer and are worth targeting until the first frosts, if the weather remains settled.

On many waters, crucians are caught at any time of day or night. I've even had good catches on blisteringly hot, calm days when nothing else bites. They don't like wind, especially when the margins are churned up, but they fill a gap when oppressive weather makes it futile to target other species. I couldn't see a summer going by without targeting these chubby chappies.

Their fighting ability, or lack of it, mirrors their sedate character. They perform a bizarre 'dance' when hooked, tipping on their side and flapping around in ever-decreasing circles until they pop to the surface. I wouldn't describe them as hard fighters and they never go off on searing runs, ripping line from the clutch. In fact, detecting crucian bites has become an art form. Anglers who target them regularly get a great sense of achievement from identifying the tiniest of indications on finely balanced pole rigs. Others have developed self-hooking bolt rigs to combat the finicky bites, which I consider horrible. I can never see myself resorting to buzzers, bobbins and bolt rigs. I tackle crucians with low-diameter lines and fine-wire hooks.

MARGINAL SWIMS

Crucians are dedicated margin feeders and love to browse along a nearside sloping shelf. The water doesn't have to be deep – some of the most productive swims are just 18in deep. They like to feed on a clear bottom close to reeds and overhanging bushes, and have an affinity with beds of lily pads, where they feed right at the edges on the abundant natural food larders.

Crucians are chiefly bottom feeders, tilting their bodies 45 degrees so that they can gently suck in morsels. They bubble over silty margins, producing

True crucians exhibit no signs of barbels around the mouth and could be less common than many think because of hybridisation.

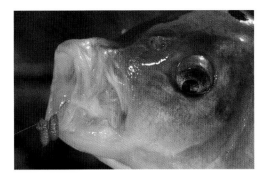

Probing the margins with sensitive pole float rigs and paste baits for the crucians that inhabit leafy Milton Lake at Bury Hill Fisheries in Surrey.

slow-moving bubbles that are larger than those generated by tench but smaller than bream's. Sometimes, it is difficult to distinguish between crucian carp bubbling and natural gases emerging from the lakebed.

Locate a swim that has a clear patch where a marginal shelf drops quickly a rod length out, and cover either side, and you have found an ideal crucian carp swim. They have a habit of rolling on the surface at any time, giving themselves away. It's almost like a tumble turn with their tail flapping away ten to the dozen as they descend quickly to the bottom. If you see one rolling on the surface, there are sure to be plenty more around, and it's unlikely they will move very far.

I try to target crucians halfway up the marginal shelf. From my own observations, they nearly always feed head facing the bank and line abreast. A friend once likened them to a row of Gillette razor blades, an apt description.

POLE FLOAT AND RUNNING LINE

For me, crucian carp fishing demands a float set-up on running line. I love fishing with a light match rod and centrepin reel – the perfect combination. I always attempt to fish the float directly below the rod tip so take 13, 15 and 20ft rods for my crucian sessions. I load my favourite Swallow centrepin with 2lb Maxima main line and a hi-tech, low-diameter hook link attached by a micro swivel.

A long, fine-tipped, tapered body pole float is my first choice, the size depending on the type of swim. The lightest rig possible produces better results. Sometimes, if there are lots of small surface rudd and roach about, you have to get the bait to the bottom quickly. I use one or two gram if small fry prove a pest.

The rig must be stable – crucians will not tolerate moving bait in a strong undertow – so add weight down the rig until stability is guaranteed. It is a balancing act since you don't want to compromise sensitivity, but with today's pole floats, olivette weights and low-diameter hook links this is rarely a problem.

One of the most important items of kit is a plummet. Wherever possible, I fish at dead-depth, only fishing over-depth if the rig skids through. With the rod placed on two rod rests and the float fished directly beneath the tip, you can concentrate on targeting the tiniest area on the sloping shelf.

A classic rig is to fish the bulk shot 12in. away from the hook, assuming that the swim is more than 3ft deep. This is where I join the hook link to the main line and place the bulk shot just above the micro swivel. In the case of an olivette, it can simply rest against the swivel. Alternatively, a string of No. 6 shot can be effective. I place at least three dropper shot on the hook link, initially evenly spaced, and possibly, if I'm looking for lift bites, moving the lower one to within a couple of inches of the hook. The dropper shot is a 10, 11 or 12 and sometimes all three in descending order with the smallest closest to the hook.

Crucian bites often barely register so you'll need a pole float, like the Fox MXP1 with its long tip.

The hook is generally a fine wire spade-end, either barbless or with a micro barb. For crucians, I prefer a relatively long-shanked hook, such as a Fox Series 3 or Kamasan B711. Hook sizes depend on bait choice but 16s, 18s and 20s usually cover all the baits I use. The float is shotted so that the very top of the tip is level with the surface of the water, or only just protruding through it. This helps to identify the tiniest bites, often signalled by a slight lifting of the float. It's rare to get tearaway bites because crucians gently suck in and blow out food items while hardly moving a fin. Use a badly shotted float and they'll do this all day long without registering a single bite. It's possible to blank in a swim that's packed with crucians.

FLEXIBLE BAITING

Baiting is one of the keys to successful crucian fishing. I try to target an area no larger than a saucer. Theoretically, even in a swim of that size, three crucians could easily be feeding side by side. I tend to think that as each fish is caught another takes its place in the same spot. It's like a conveyor belt – get the baiting right and you can have them queuing up all day.

A small baitdropper is the best way of ensuring that the feed is kept in a tight area and goes straight to the bottom without being intercepted by surface-feeding roach and rudd. Alternatively, hard balls of groundbait about the size of a walnut can be thrown tight against the rod tip. It's surprising how little feed you need to keep a shoal of crucians going all day. I normally start with six walnut-sized balls of groundbait or two small baitdropper loads of freebies. If I can avoid it, I will not put in any free-falling bait, either by hand or catapult, because this will disperse into a much larger area and you never know how much is being eaten by other species feeding higher in the water.

I normally take a good selection of bait and ring the changes until I discover the fish's preference. This may change throughout the day, so don't be too dogmatic. My favourite baits are red maggots, casters, mini pellets, hemp, sweetcorn and specialist pastes. I even use combinations of these baits, including corn and paste tipped with maggots, and paste studded with pellets.

Any indication on the float that looks out of the ordinary warrants a strike. Don't expect the float to sail away or rise from the water. When the float doesn't act as it should, a firm lift of the rod tip often meets solid resistance.

I expect immediate action if crucians are in the swim. Avoid leaving the rig in place longer than a couple of minutes. Fishing a tight area, it's possible for crucians to bury your bait or lie with their body on top of it. Every couple of minutes, I ease the rig out of the water and gently replace it an inch or so to the left or right, and this often provokes an immediate response.

Crucians don't mind the odd ball of groundbait or baitdropper being lowered among them. I top up the swim at 30-minute intervals, but you should let the action dictate your feed rate. With crucians, it's best to err on the side of caution.

Sit farther back from the water's edge than normal because crucians are easily spooked from the margins by excessive movement on the bank.

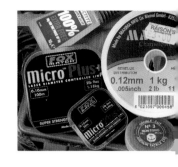

ABOVE: **A spool of 2lb Maxima is a dependable choice across numerous species but for tricky crucians you'll probably benefit from a low-diameter hook trace.**

RIGHT: **If a crucian fills the bottom of your net like this there's every chance it could spin the scales to 4lb.**

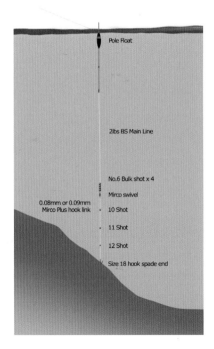

Pole float rig.

9 Chub

I'S NEVER TOO HOT OR TOO COLD for chub to feed. They are worth targeting in summer droughts and raging winter floods on rivers, lakes, pits and reservoirs countrywide. Chub take advantage of any food item and have been caught on a wider variety of baits than any other species. They are regularly taken on livebaits, deadbaits, artificial lures, flies and natural baits, such as slugs, worms and maggots, as well as carp pellets and boilies.

The chub has always played second fiddle in popularity to the barbel but is edging much closer to its whiskered rival following a marked increase in its size and distribution. A 6-pounder used to be the fish of a lifetime, but hundreds of chub of this size are now reported every year, and this has become the new specimen standard. Seven-pounders are no longer a rarity and monsters over 8lb have been caught from numerous rivers including the Thames, Dorset Stour and Kennet. The British record has ballooned to 9lb 4oz, taken from a pond known as Greenmire, linked to the River Thames. The fact that I was privileged to see this fish will remain one of the highlights of my angling career.

I predict that more 9-pounders will emerge in future seasons. In fact, I believe that 10-pounders probably already exist and it is only a matter of time before one is caught and raises the bar even higher. Global warming, highly nutritious anglers' baits and the abundance of signal crayfish have all been cited as possible causes.

Chub spawn between April and June, depending on conditions and water temperature, and are amazingly good at reproducing. They are naturally fish of river systems but there is ample evidence that they also spawn successfully in stillwaters. Several weeks beforehand, male chub start to display spawning tubercles – small, grey bumps that are easier to feel than to see – under the skin around their heads, gill covers and pectoral fins. In rivers, chub spawn among the stones in shallow runs and often head up side-streams, brooks and tributaries. On stillwaters, they have been observed spawning like carp among overhanging branches. They become aggressive at this time of the year and bear battle scars after spawning.

This undercut bank on Rolf's Lake near Oxford, acts as a big chub sanctuary. The fish migrated into the lake during floods and they've grown to 8lb.

MAGIC MIX

Chub are slow growing, reaching about 9in. in length by their third year, when they become sexually mature. They are thought to live for 12 or 15 years, possibly not so long where rapid weight gain shortens their lifespan. Many Oxford gravel pits have contained giant chub for years but rivers have caught up and record-breakers could be taken from either habitat.

On rivers, chub spend many weeks after spawning cleaning themselves in the shallows. They head for the fastest runs where there is plenty of oxygen and a continual stream of food. The shoals are often quite dense and big bags are possible as long as you don't spook them by catching or losing a fish before they are on the bait. Spend time introducing a stream of small baits, such as maggots, hemp and casters, and the chub shoal will become very competitive. Then it's possible to extract all the fish in a shoal.

My favourite mix is a 50–50 helping of hemp and casters. I've yet to find any other baits to beat this magic combo. Hemp and casters drop through the swim quicker than maggots and become trapped between stones, provoking chub to root them out. Another key benefit of these baits is that they are less likely than maggots to be battered by the minnow hordes.

It requires a lot of bait to work up chub, especially if the shoal contains between 10 and 20 individuals. As much as a gallon of hemp and casters might be needed over a five-hour session.

I'd recommend a short Loafer or Chubber float for this approach, teamed with the lightest line possible and an ultra strong, size 18 spade-end hook. Wherever possible, I fish 2lb line straight through, and providing you dictate the fight, even monster chub can be landed on this light gear.

FEEDING TACTICS

Many early season swims are weedy, and it is impossible to pull chub upstream through the foliage. Plan in advance where to land the fish by placing your landing net well downstream. Then play chub down with the current, making it easier to keep them free of weed.

In swims that are not suitable for trotting, a small block-end feeder is a great alternative. Again, stealthy feeding is required because hooking a fish on the first cast spooks the rest. I make a dozen casts without a hook link to get the chub used to the splash of the feeder entering the water. Keep casting the feeder filled with bait until they attack it on the bottom in their

Spray hemp and casters, and chub make pigs of themselves.

Long, solid stems on these Fox Avons also make them suitable for swift swims.

eagerness to feed. Once they start to do this, attach a short hook link of 2in. and you should be in business.

Being able to see the shoal is a huge advantage – if you can't, it's easy to overestimate the number of fish and overbait the swim, making it impossible to hit bites. What happens is that the chub charge around and chase bait downstream as freebies start to elude them. The aim is to feed just sufficient so no free offerings drift any farther than a couple of yards past the point of impact. This guarantees confident, easy to hit bites.

The method works well on clear, medium-sized rivers, but small streams present different problems. Shoals in these venues are much smaller and might consist of just six fish. By the time you spot them, they have already seen you and it's game over. In summer, the solution is to use floating breadcrust. Scatter a few crusts on the surface and allow them to drift downstream. Keep a sensible distance and you should spot chub rising up to take the crusts before there is any danger of them being spooked. Once located, creep into position well upstream and trot a free-lined cube of crust through to their doorstep.

This type of fishing requires heavy cover, which is no place for light lines and match rods. An Avon-style 12-footer with a 1lb test curve is perfect matched with 6lb line so that you can muscle a big chub from the undergrowth. A heavy duty, size 4, eyed hook suits this operation.

Floating crust also allows you to locate chub that are completely out of sight in long tunnels of reeds and through the thickest undergrowth. Just listen for them slurping the crust down! It's a fantastic method on a warm summer's evening and at night.

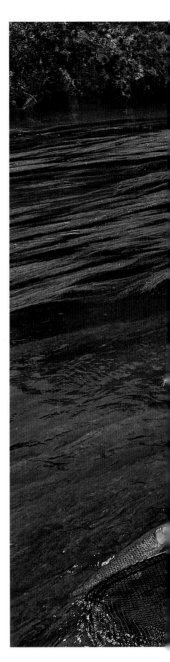

This Hampshire Avon chub was hooked in a clear gravel run at the far bank and surfed across river through thick weed.

BAIT FOR SOLITARY FISH

As the days shorten and temperatures fall, chub shoals disperse and fish move into deeper reaches of the river. It's now that mature fish often become solitary and tough to target. These big chub are more likely to fall to barbel tactics with pellets and boilies. I still try to fish as light as possible, but anticipate that I might hook a barbel. For that reason, I use 6lb fluorocarbon straight through, which is a good compromise. It won't spook most chub and still gives you a realistic chance of landing a bonus barbel.

I use a baitdropper to lay a small bed of mini pellets and broken boilies in one tight spot. A semi-fixed, in-line leger rig is all that's needed. Unlike barbel, chub rarely hook themselves, particularly on a hair-rig. They have a frustrating habit of pulling the tip around without the hook taking hold. I find it best to fish a short hair, or even side hook a boilie or banded pellet. Sit close to the rod and strike at any positive takes you get. It's unusual to get more than three fish in a single session, but it's a classic way of targeting individual fish that have been previously located.

Baitdroppers are capable of switching on a swim by thoroughly carpeting the gravels in double quick time. It's also worth baiting a sleeper swim nearby, which can be checked periodically for signs of activity.

Some of these deeper glides can also be attacked with a float. A straight peacock waggler is a great choice, and you can certainly drop right down on the diameter of the line. Steadily feed the swim with a mixture of casters, hemp and micro pellets via a baitdropper.

During periods of heavy floods, large smelly baits are effective. This is a good time to use traditional offerings, including Canadian Cheddar, which is ultra reliable and you don't need to do anything to it. The cheese is easily moulded around a size 4 hook, leaving the point showing for a better hook up.

At this time of the year, I often fish around overhanging trees, deeply undercut banks and large eddies. No freebies are needed – a big chunk of cheese is sufficient to draw the chub to your hook bait. Give each swim 30 minutes before moving on. If a chub is at home, action is normally instant, so it pays to travel light.

Cheese is my preferred bait at flood-time but worms, bread and flavoured luncheon meat are also worth considering, particularly as colour starts to fade from the river.

An old warrior of a chub scaling 6lb 7oz hooked from Rolf's Lake near Oxford. Andy had five chub topping 6lb in the same session on pole float and maggots from a deeply undercut bank.

MAGGOTS FOR WINTER

When the first frosts arrive and rivers run low and clear with reduced cover, maggot fishing is the preferred method – and you will still need plenty of bait. The chub join up again in calm, deeper glides, ideally flanked by shallow gravels at either end.

Feed a steady stream of maggots before you even think about setting up. At this time of the year, I arrive on the bank before dawn and sit on my box catapulting a dozen maggots every 30 seconds for a good hour. Many of my best winter catches have come with this approach. I still use a 2lb main line but drop down to a low-diameter, hi-tech hook link and size 20 hook with a single maggot. My favourite hook-link material is Fox Micro Plus, 0.09 or 0.10mm in diameter, joined to the main line by a micro swivel.

A bottle of glycerine is essential on frosty mornings – if the temperature remains below freezing all day, the line may freeze in the tiny rings of a match rod. Smear a small amount of glycerine around each ring beforehand and the line should flow freely for hours. Once the glycerine wears off, dry the rings and reapply.

I like to use a straight peacock waggler because these are less affected with the line buried. More importantly, they make far less noise on the strike than a float fished top and bottom. In these tricky conditions, a splashy strike could spook a shoal of wary chub. Traditionally, river chub weigh heaviest right at the end of the season.

There's barely enough light to see the float on a frosty dawn at Throop, but a big chub has thumped the rod tip and made its intentions plain.

STILLWATER TARGETS

Stillwater chub are now accepted as legitimate targets. Many anglers think chub have inhabited stillwaters for just a short time, but I caught my first one in the early 1960s from Sabby's gravel pit in West Drayton. We used to catch a lot of them on floating breadcrust in summer when we were after carp. Big chub also do well in ponds, reservoirs and canals after migrating from rivers during floods. For many years it was thought that chub couldn't spawn in stillwaters, but breeding has occurred in some venues. Six-pounders are common and eight stillwaters have produced fish over 8lb. A reputed 10lb chub has been landed from a lake but wasn't authenticated.

My favourite stillwaters are the vast gravel pits in Oxfordshire, where monsters have lurked for many years. In the past, they proved difficult to target and were rarely caught. One of the successful methods was to free-line sardines in the margins on a wintry night. This still produces chub, but there are much easier ways to catch them nowadays. They love coming into very shallow water at night, especially when a strong wind blows a lot of food to one end of the pit.

One way of locating big chub on large gravel pits is to search for them at night with a strong torch. Many of these waters are crystal clear, and providing there's no bankside activity to deter them, chub often swim into the margins, where the water barely covers their backs. It's surprising what you can see by creeping around and illuminating the margins.

Modern methods have changed the face of stillwater chubbing. Even sparsely stocked waters can be fished with a high degree of confidence using maggots. Stillwater chub like to cruise near the surface throughout the year but especially in winter, and they respond remarkably well to sprayed maggots. They can spot free-falling maggots from a considerable distance, probably using both sight and sound.

Stillwater chub rarely follow the maggots down. Even in 20ft of water, they resolutely remain in the top 3ft, ignoring bait that has drifted down any deeper. This means it is quite hard to overbait. Feed on a little-and-often basis and try to pick three markers on the far bank so you can accurately catapult the free offerings to three different spots, ideally about 30ft apart. This keeps the chub circulating, and when you hook a fish the rest of the shoal is more likely to move to one of the other spots rather than drifting away altogether.

The rich gravel pits ringing Oxford have long had a reputation for growing outsize chub. Among them is Hardwick on the day ticket Richworth Linear complex.

SPRAYING MAGGOTS

Fine, well-balanced tackle is essential for spraying maggots – I use a 13ft match rod and small fixed-spool reel loaded with 2lb line. Again, I like to attach a separate hook link of 18in., ideally of 0.09mm diameter Micro Plus. This is virtually invisible and is terminated with a fairly strong size 20 hook that will hold one or two maggots. I position a suitably sized loaded waggler directly above a micro swivel joining the main line and hook link, holding it in place with a couple of locking shots. I don't include any weight on the hook link so the bait falls naturally through the surface layers.

The key thing is to keep the bait going in to keep the chub's attention. I carry on baiting even while playing fish if I'm sure others are in the area. This is an amazingly successful method and has even accounted for monsters, which only exist in very small numbers in big expanses of water. Where there is a good stocking of chub, it's absolutely devastating and multiple bags are easy to achieve.

Another method worthy of consideration on stillwaters is to fish with scaled-down carp rigs. Chub get used to carp anglers' boilies and pellets continually raining in, and although very few are hooked on carp gear, because of the way they feed, they certainly feast on the freebies. Fish for them with an Avon rod, 5 or 6lb main line and a 4lb hook link on a running rig and the results are potentially astounding.

The ideal set-up for this approach is a size 14 hook with a hair-rigged mini boilie strapped tight against it. Banded pellets and side-hook boilies also work extremely well. Identifying bites is the key to success. I like to fish a running leger with a 6in. hook link and lightweight bobbins. I strike at any positive indication instead of waiting for a screaming take. Pop-ups are fished in the same way and at times prove even more successful. Fishing this rig over a bed of mini boilies and pellets in a shallow bay is very rewarding.

GRAND UNION CANAL

Canals are often overlooked but chub living in these venues have also grown in size. The Grand Union Canal produces 6-pounders from several areas, and the odd 7-pounder has been recorded. Most are caught in matches on a long pole under far bank cover, so it's worth keeping an eye on the *Angler's Mail* match pages. Many hot swims are well known and consistently produce chub.

A friend has done well using mini boilies, micro pellets and artificial casters hair-rigged on a light leger set-up and dropped beneath far-bank cover with a pole pot attached to a long pole. This gives accurate baiting in tight areas that are impossible to cast to using gear that's strong enough to extract big chub.

We've never had it so good for big chub and I just hope the trend continues.

Christchurch river guide Chris Holley and a 6lb 10oz chub from his home waters on the Dorset Stour.

RIGHT: **Large rudd feed within easy wading range of the bank at Frensham small pond as they migrate in and out of the reed-bed food larders.**

BELOW: **Maggots and mini pellets figure high on the rudd menu.**

10 Rudd

Golden flanks and bright red fins give the rudd a vivid, striking appearance, but despite these glowing colours, it is frequently confused with the more silvery roach. Generally, the rudd's body shape is much deeper than the roach's. Another key indicator is that the first ray of the rudd's dorsal fin is always set behind the pelvic fins, whereas on a roach it's almost level. The rudd's mouth is clearly upturned because the fish has evolved into a dedicated surface feeder, unlike the roach. The iris of the eye is also completely different. The rudd's has a much lighter colouration, appearing yellow to orange, while the roach's is distinctly darker and more crimson. Finally, the rudd has fewer lateral-line scales than the roach – 42 compared with as many as 49 on the roach.

Rudd are widely distributed in all kinds of waters from weedy farm ponds to vast gravel pits, canals, meres and drains. Some of the biggest specimens live in large Irish loughs, but they are rarely targeted.

Slow-growing rudd reach a length of 3in. in their second season and survive for around 15 years. Their growth rates have shown little change for decades and a fish of 2lb is still classed as a specimen. Three-pounders are very rare and 4lb plus fish are the maximum size you are ever likely to find.

Juvenile rudd feed mainly on zooplankton, gradually stepping up their diet to soft water plants and filamentous algae. As they start to mature, they also dine on emerging insects and tiny pea snails. They are summer fish and enter a semi-dormant state for much of the winter, which is why they are so slow growing. They feed in earnest only when the temperature is quite high.

A glittering rudd from Frensham Small Pond. Pure, clear waters always enhance their golden sheen.

LOCATING SHOALS

Rudd are one of my favourite species in conditions of blistering heat and flat calm. They feed when nothing else stirs in the shallowest, warmest water. They are confirmed shoal fish and, because year-classes stay together, it's not unusual to locate groups of similar-sized rudd. Shoals of juveniles contain thousands of fish, but it's rare to find large specimens in groups of more than a dozen.

Most of my rudd fishing involves trying to locate these smaller shoals of giant rudd. Having found them, it is nerve-racking trying to catch one. I feed floating baits until the rudd show interest. Never cast at them until they are on the feed.

Steamy session in the shallows. The challenge is finding a way through many thousands of smaller rudd to place a bait in front of 2lb plus specimens.

You will probably get just a single chance so it's always prudent to try to hook the largest before the rest spook. I think their extreme wariness has evolved because they are always on the lookout for predators. Perch and small pike constantly prey on juvenile rudd, and even the largest rudd are not safe from the jaws of a big pike.

Unfortunately, where rudd, roach and bream are found in the same venue, there is every chance they will hybridise. Depending on the location of the water, spawning normally occurs in April or May and naturally the fish will be at their heaviest just before this time. The best chance of locating a 3-pounder is from late March through to the end of April.

Big rudd thrive on neglect and for the specialist angler it's always worth investigating lightly fished venues. Large gravel pits and meres with shallow bays that quickly warm up are a great starting point, especially as many are gin-clear, making it much easier to spot specimens. Don't be too concerned if the shallows contain mere inches of water – the biggest rudd often move into margins where the depth barely covers their body. If lily pads and reeds are to be found in the vicinity, so much the better, because these hold natural food larders for rudd, and they love to forage among cover where the temperature rises as in an oven.

Remote fens and moorland drains are potential specimen rudd haunts. In contrast, there are carp venues where big rudd thrive and grow to specimen proportions without being noticed. Very occasionally, a giant rudd falls to a carp angler's bait and it's worth asking around to see if this has happened. Unbelievably, these big rudd are rarely weighed because they are regarded as a nuisance.

BAITS FOR CAUTIOUS FEEDERS

All my rudd fishing is concentrated in the top few inches of water with either a surface bait or a slow-sinking one. Floating casters, maggots and mini pellets head my bait requirements, and I particularly like high-quality, floating koi pellets, which are sold in several different sizes.

Regular feeding with small helpings of freebies usually attracts a response, but it's always best to err on the side of caution as you'll want to avoid overbaiting a swim. Big rudd are cautious feeders and cruise around slowly, gently sipping in floating freebies.

Small hooks and low-diameter lines are essential to avoid spooking shy rudd. I use a soft-tipped waggler rod and small fixed-spool reel loaded with 2lb line. A low-diameter, hi-tech hook link gives you an edge, and I add a tiny controller or specialist surface waggler for casting weight.

Rudd boil in the surface film at Frensham Small Pond on a mid-summer morning. Fish over 4lb are known to have died of old age without being caught in the shallow, sandy mere.

You need to use your eyes to judge when to strike at a take – don't be in too much of a hurry. If big rudd are easily observed, give them a moment to ensure that they have sucked in the bait confidently and have not just tested it. A premature strike will only spook the fish.

Rudd love floating breadcrust and one of the great traditional methods of catching them is to tether a chunk of stale loaf to a stone at the edge of a reed-bed and watch fish simply peck away at it. Sometimes you can attract four or five rudd at a time around the chunk of bread and then just cast a fingernail-sized piece of free-lined crust close to them.

It's more of a problem selecting specimen rudd on overstocked waters that contain fish of all sizes. Although you may be able to locate small pods of large fish, as soon as you introduce bait, thousands of juveniles race in like piranhas. This happens on venues such as the Carp Society's Horseshoe Lake and Frensham Small Pond, but it is still possible to adopt a selective approach.

A mini boilie suspended a foot below a waggler float easily distracts the tiny rudd, giving you an opportunity to target the bigger fish. In these cases, I feed a mixture of free offerings – maggots and hemp to keep the tiny rudd occupied and mini boilies for the bigger fish. On occasions, I have increased the size of the bait to 14mm, which big rudd readily accept on carp lakes.

Mostly, rudd swim within easy casting range but occasionally, where access to large, shallow bays is limited, you may be forced to fish at longer range. Specimen rudd can still be targeted on a leger rig using small pieces of suspended crust, or even a tiny pop-up boilie. I tie up a rig with the hook link set as close as possible to the depth of the swim, fishing the buoyant bait directly above a free-running leger weight. It doesn't seem to matter if the bait is on the surface or just below – either is acceptable. I still fish fine, using a light feeder rod, 3lb main line and hi-tech low-diameter hook link with a fine-wire hook. Binoculars prove useful in these swims because they allow you to observe the bait at long range. I set up the rods on buzzers with lightweight bobbins. Surprisingly, takes are very positive, especially if you can cast the rig close to reeds or lily pads.

ABOVE: **Andy knows that the biggest rudd in Frensham Small Pond are often hooked on boilies by carp anglers. So he targets them on float gear with a small, soft boilie mounted directly on a size 14 hook. He pulls the hook into the boilie with a baiting needle until only the point shows.**

LEFT: **Horseshoe Lake rudd hooked on red maggots. The species grows to more than 3lb in the 62-acre Cotswolds gravel pit.**

DRY-FLY FISHING

Rudd are rarely tackled with a fly rod, but they readily accept floating and emerging insects and this approach could prove more successful than many anglers realise. I suggest a light outfit with a No. 4 floating line and fine tippet. Size 18 or 20 dry flies, such as Black Gnats and Grey Dusters, would be my first choice. Cast to individually rising fish as the light fades at dusk. Tiny emerging patterns and spent shuck imitations are worth considering. With this approach, you could cover a lot of water in a short time, especially on drains, dykes and canals, where most of the rudd will be found surface feeding against the far banks. I know that dry-fly anglers on Irish loughs have hooked huge rudd by mistake over brown trout lies.

Although most of my rudd fishing is concentrated around the surface, there are times when big rudd can be caught on the bottom in deeper swims. This is something that I rarely do, because generally there are other species to go after in such conditions, but when the temperature soars and the atmospheric pressure rises producing a flat calm, I doubt there's a better species worth hunting than rudd.

Wading out among the rudd with a bait waiter and plentiful supplies of feed to prevent the shoals drifting away.

11 Perch

THINK IT WAS THE LATE DICK WALKER who described the pugnacious perch as our 'biggest looking, large fish'. I know what he meant, for the profile of a specimen perch belies its true weight. A 4lb plus perch looks enormous due to its short, deep body, huge head and massive, sail-like dorsal fin. Together with its bold, vertical stripes and blood-red fins, it is a truly individual coarse fish.

The perch has made a miraculous recovery from a devastating population crash in the 1970s, caused by a virulent disease. The species is now widespread again in all water types, and perch have especially taken advantage of high stock densities and habitat conditions in carp-bagging waters. Small commercial pools that are coloured like weak tea, allow perch to feed non-stop and make the most of regular carp spawnings.

A 3-pounder is the target for most specialists, and fish of this weight are catchable all year round, despite the perch being slightly heavier before spawning. In fact, a fish weighing over 4lb is becoming a realistic target and a 5lb plus specimen is not the pipedream it used to be. There has been a slow increase in the upper size of perch as the UK species approaches the size of fish caught regularly in mainland Europe. Many specialists believe that a perch of 6lb will emerge shortly.

Perch are relatively short-lived compared to most other fish species, and rarely survive beyond nine years, usually failing to reach seven. However, where prey stocks are abundant and perch numbers are not excessive, they show amazing growth. Overstocking is always a problem with perch – it's not unusual for them to spawn so successfully that they overpopulate a water and become stunted. When they first find their way into a fishery, perch quickly become monsters because their numbers are relatively low. These big fish are often caught for several seasons before disappearing and being replaced by thousands of smaller ones. This is the reason why popular perch waters are here today and gone tomorrow. Getting the best out of specimen venues requires precise timing, and it is imperative that you find current information about a perch venue instead of relying on historical records. Perch waters that were famous for huge specimens years ago, now rarely produce fish over 1lb. Luckily, plenty of venues don't fall into this category, especially rivers, large pits and reservoirs, where more balanced stock levels can be maintained.

COLOURS AND HABITS

Perch tolerate the coldest conditions and, unlike many species, are at home in very deep water. They also survive in brackish conditions, successfully populating many tidal reaches. They spawn early in the year, usually March or April, and this is when the largest specimens are caught,

despite their unpredictable feeding habits. One minute, big perch may seize sizeable livebaits, dragging under large floats used with heavy pike gear, while the next, you'll be struggling to hook the tiniest perch bite on fine pole gear with a single maggot!

The colours of adult perch change, depending on water clarity. In clear pits and rivers, they display beautiful olive-green flanks, near black stripes and blood-red fins. On highly-stained carp-bagging waters, the colours are washed out with faint bar markings and orange rather than red fins. In extreme cases, I've known the body colouration to resemble that of lightly coloured tench.

Perch are ambush feeders and lie deep in cover waiting for an easy meal to pass their doorstep. They favour sunken branches, landing stages, mooring posts and old wooden bridges. In clear conditions, a shoal of big perch may be

Perch, like this 2lb 9oz prickly specimen, prosper in small streams like the Surrey Wey, on a diet of minnows and sticklebacks.

observed hanging like Christmas decorations among the submerged branches of bushes and trees. Concrete structures are another favourite location and they lie tight against walls, lock cuttings and weirs.

On reservoirs, monster perch inhabit very deep water, especially around valve towers. I've caught them as far down as 30ft, and on the Continent I know waters where they have been caught 10ft deeper than that. Big perch are rarely found in wide, open expanses with an even depth, unless there is plenty of weed cover. Although small perch are happy to adopt the long chase approach to hunting prey, specimen perch are older and wiser and won't waste energy on a long, drawn-out pursuit. A cunning ambush is their ploy.

Perch have fantastic eyesight and in clear water shy away from thick lines and poorly presented baits. The best feeding times are first thing in the morning and at dusk, when light levels are low and they can use their keen sight to its best advantage.

RIGHT: Full stretch for a 2lb perch at Longham Waterworks on the Dorset Stour.

BELOW: Lock cuttings on the lower Thames are full of snags, including supermarket trolleys, but perch appreciate such cover to ambush their prey.

VARIED TACTICS

Due to their gregarious nature, perch are caught on a wide range of tactics, encompassing everything from live and deadbaits, artificial flies and lures, to maggots, worms and casters.

Specimen perch waters are extremely varied and tactics as well as baits change between venues. I have never seriously targeted perch with large live or deadbaits, but on rivers a small gudgeon or minnow is my first choice in summer. Lip-hooking a minnow on a size 6 hook and fishing it below a Loafer float is a classic approach. Trot this free-roving rig downstream and you'll cover a lot of water. It's also a brilliant set-up for weir-pools, allowing the bait to work around eddies and directly below the weir-sill. Loafer or Chubber floats carry between one and five swanshot, depending on the size of bait, depth of swim and speed of current.

Although free-roving bait also works in stillwaters, I prefer to paternoster a small livebait. This is particularly effective near snags or structures because it prevents the bait being hung up. A buoyant Chubber or even a small bob float will suspend a rig directly above a leger weight of between 0.8 to 1oz. A short, rotary hook link is positioned so it fishes just off the bottom. The hook link should be no more than 6in. in length and the livebait tail-hooked so that it is continually swimming away from the rig to avoid tangles.

A lip-hooked minnow is deadly for perch on rivers and the same size of hook will also take a bunch of maggots.

It's worth keeping an eye out for shoals of big perch ambushing fry. The tiny fish scatter on the surface in fright as they are pushed upwards by the big stripeys below. Perch attack their prey in a co-ordinated pack. Drop your livebait among the fleeing fry and you could well be in business.

Roving with a lure rod has long been a standard perch tactic in both summer and winter. Top patterns are tiny spoons and spinners on a light outfit. A new lure method that is gaining in popularity is vertical jigging using small rubber shads. The shads have a lead head on which the body is mounted. This is basically a large single hook with a heavily weighted eye, usually resembling a fish head. The soft rubber body is mounted on the hook and fished tight to the bottom in short jigging motions. These lures can also be cast around snags without fear of getting caught up because they fish with the point of the hook uppermost.

Shads of between 3 and 4in. in length are ideal for targeting specimen perch. This approach works well both from the bank and from the boat and is ideal for exploring around bridges, weirs and other obstacles. Specialist jigging rods have been developed with very fast tapers and stiff tips, making it far easier to introduce action into the lure. This is further enhanced by non-stretch braids, which also help bite detection because you are in constant touch with the lure.

The pulsating action of rubbery Chubby Shads plays on the aggressive instincts of perch.

CHOPPED WORMS AND CASTERS

Lobworms are the traditional perch bait, but smaller Dendrobaenas, redworms and even tiny bloodworm all play a role. One of the finest attractors for perch is chopped worm introduced in a baitdropper tight to the bottom. These chopped pieces have amazing pulling power and perch pick up the scent from quite some distance away.

Although small perch are greedy feeders and quickly swallow your bait, the same isn't true of big perch. Despite their huge mouths, they can give the most delicate of bites even on low-diameter lines and tiny hooks. My first 4lb perch, caught in the depths of winter, fell to a pole-float rig with a size 20 hook and half a small Dendrobaena worm. The bite barely registered on the float.

For delicate presentation, I like to fish directly below the rod tip. My first choice main line is 2lb Maxima with a hi-tech hook link of 0.09mm Fox Micro Plus. Choice of hook is also critical. My preference is a fine-wire hook but it needs to be strong, and the Kamasan B611 falls into this category. Even with baits as big as half a lobworm I still use a small hook, usually no larger than a 14 and often as small as a 20.

Casters have caught me a lot of big perch in recent years. Perch like crunching on the crisp-shelled baits. The combination of casters and chopped worm gives you an edge on tough days. One of my favourite methods is to fish a couple of casters on a size 16 hook at dead depth over finely chopped worms, including bloodworm if I can get hold of them. A long-tipped, delicate pole float gives you the best chance of registering tentative bites. Fishing directly below the rod tip aids accuracy, especially when feeding with a baitdropper.

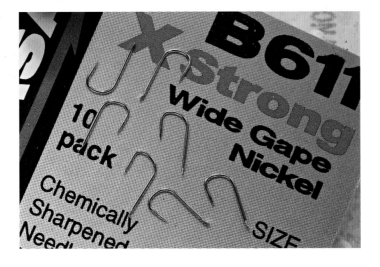

The Kamasan B611 with its wide gape and needle sharp point will penetrate the hard mouth of a large perch.

These tactics are ideally suited to stillwaters and places such as lock cuttings and canals. Rivers, including the Thames, have come on in leaps and bounds in recent years and can be tackled in a similar manner by using a small Avon float to register bites.

LONG-RANGE FEEDER RIG

In reservoirs and gravel pits, perch are often targeted at long range with feeder gear. In these circumstances, a mix of red maggots and worms is hard to beat. I normally set up light feeder rods with 3 or 4lb line and short, hi-tech hook links fished paternoster-style above the feeder, which is usually a block-end.

If regulations allow, I use two hook links so I can fish one with maggots and the other with worms. The hook links are 3–4in. in length with a micro swivel on one end and the hook on the other. The micro swivels are trapped between a couple of rubber float stops, which allows for adjustment above the block-end attached to the main line.

The finely chopped worms and maggots packed into the feeder leak out attractive juices to pull in the big perch. Two red maggots fished on a size 18 is my first line of attack.

On these venues, I fish against an underwater feature where there is a rapid change in depth. Islands, gravel bars, plateaux and peninsulars are all potential hotspots. Time spent checking the depths is worthwhile, and wherever possible I like to fish at the bottom of a steep drop-off. Perch congregate in these zones, and the more rapid the change in depth, the better.

Once I've located one of these spots, I mark its position on the main line with a small fold of electrical tape or short length of distance-marker braid. I always aim to keep casting on exactly the same spot so the contents of the feeder gradually build up the swim and continue to draw more perch into the area with each cast.

For bite indication, I use light bobbins and buzzers. Where multiple rods are allowed, I try several potential hotspots rather than putting all my eggs in one basket.

EXPERIMENTING WITH BAITS

Big perch have a habit of suddenly starting to feed after several biteless hours. Fish may have been in the swim throughout this time, but once the feeding switch is thrown, several bites often come in succession. I think a lot of this has to do with light intensity and atmospheric pressure.

I have been experimenting by adding spicy and fishy boilie flavours to my baits when feeder fishing with maggots and worms. I either add flavours directly to the bait or inject them into a sponge, which I push inside the feeder. Rather than going for high-strength flavours, I use boilie dips. Best results have come from a 50–50 combination of Richworth Crab and Mussel and the new K-G-1.

Suspended or popped-up baits occasionally outfish standard bottom baits. Air-injected lobworms have accounted for many big perch over the years. Artificial, buoyant casters and maggots from Enterprise Tackle also work. I like to fish one artificial grub with at least one natural. The distance they are suspended off the bottom varies, but a couple of inches is about right. With an air-injected lobworm you may need a small split-shot to set the depth correctly, but with a paternoster rig on a short hook link there is no need. This is also a useful method over weed and snags. A running paternoster with a leger link of about 6in. and hook link of 18in. provides brilliant presentation, ensuring that the hook bait isn't buried in weed or debris.

Although perch can be fished all year, my favourite time is deepest winter; they are reliable targets even when a hard frost crunches underfoot.

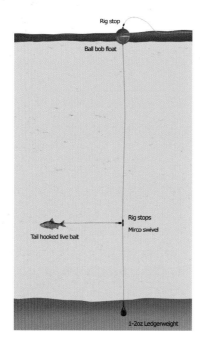

Livebait paternoster rig.

The drop-off formed by a deep water channel running close to the bank is prime perch territory.

RIGHT: A 40lb English common is the ultimate target for many carp anglers. Andy achieved the ambition at Wintons fishery in West Sussex when he stalked this 44lb beauty, known as Wood Carving, with a floating trout pellet. (Photo: Greg Meenehan/ *Angler's Mail*)

BELOW: Micron EOS alarms incorporate the latest digital technology. A remote receiver mimics exactly what is going on in the head.

12 Carp

CARP ARE THE NATION'S CULT FISH with the greatest following. They have inspired more tackle, bait and tactical developments than any other species. Some anglers claim that carp have single-handedly saved the tackle trade and changed the face of modern coarse fishing. Ironically, it wasn't that long ago that carp hunting was branded a waste of time. They were portrayed as uncatchable, apart from during a limited period in early summer when they basked on the surface. How times have changed!

Wherever you live in the UK, you won't be far from a 20lb carp. A fish of that weight used to be a milestone in most carp anglers' careers but these days they barely warrant a second look. A 20-pounder is still prestigious but the bar has been moved so high that most specialists target 30lb plus.

The carp record has catapulted from 44 to more than 60lb over the years that I have fished for them. Once the carp bug has struck, most specialists become totally absorbed in the species. It's thought that carp devotion is a prime cause of many divorces.

You don't always need brute power with carp. Andy played out five 20-pounders during a day's tench session on Horseshoe Lake using his barbel rods and 6lb line.

DIFFERENTIATING CARP

Developments on the UK carp scene influence the rest of Europe. The compulsive appeal of the species is simply due to the fact that they are the largest native freshwater fish after catfish. Specialist carp fisheries are located throughout the country, from the Highlands of Scotland to Dover.

Carp are unique in their appearance and the king carp, which is the group descriptive name, comprises a number of different scale patterns. There are two fully scaled varieties, one with small, uniform scales covering its entire body, known as a common carp, while a fully scaled mirror has larger, more irregular shaped patterns. Leather carp have no scales at all and are sometimes known as the nude variety.

Two more scale patterns make up the set. A scattered scale mirror has scales of various sizes haphazardly positioned all over the body, but the most

RIGHT: **This 25lb mirror sipped a Mixer from the waves at West Stow Lake near Bury St Edmunds.**

BELOW: **Stratos carp reel with 60mm diameter spool for long casting, slow oscillating gearing for neat line lay, smooth front clutch and micro-adjustable free-spool system.**

appealing variety is the linear mirror, which normally has one row of uniformly sized scales along the entire length of the lateral line. Sometimes, there's a second row along the back, just below the dorsal fin. Unique variations in scale pattern make individual fish easy to identify, and regular visitors to the bank invariably end up with nationally famous nicknames.

Carp are hardy, long-lived fish and reproduce very well. Spawning takes place from May to July and can happen more than once during this period. In the right environment, they display phenomenal growth rates, possibly reaching 20lb in their fourth or fifth year. Individual fish have been known to survive for 60 years although 40 is probably a more realistic lifespan. Carp have the amazing ability to put on a spurt in their growth rate, even well into maturity. It's almost as if they freewheel for a considerable time and then suddenly accelerate, often doubling their bulk. There are also tremendous annual fluctuations in weight. Females carrying heavy spawn are one factor, but some carp go on a feeding spree as winter approaches, packing on the pounds to see them through the months when food may be less abundant and becoming lighter again by spring.

Many experts predict that we will see the first 70lb carp within the next few years. Never in my wildest dreams did I think that a UK water could produce such leviathans. We are catching up fast with France, Germany and Italy, which are the traditional homes of monster carp. Big carp on the Continent are not doing so badly either and I believe there will always be slightly larger fish on the other side of the Channel for those who want to hunt them.

CARP FISHING VENUES

In the early years of carp fishing, the fish were thought to become semi-dormant or hibernate in winter. There could have been some truth in this theory, despite the fact that they are now caught all year round. The reasons for the change in their cold-water feeding habits are partly the influence of anglers providing regular supplies of food and partly climatic changes.

Finding a local carp water is never a problem. The species prospers in every type of venue from the tiniest ponds to massive reservoirs, small and large rivers, canals and drains. With such a huge following, specialist carp waters are springing up almost overnight. These range from the proverbial hole in the ground with barely a feature to beautifully landscaped waters with fluctuating depths, islands, bars and all types of water plants. Stocking levels vary hugely. Some of the more productive specimen waters started out as bagging pools, where the fish have grown too large for the match angler, and the specialists have moved in.

Stalking among the pads where a big fish was spotted moments earlier burying its head in silt to siphon out bloodworm.

Certain waters have been stocked with the classic Leney strain, which are long, almost lean, chestnut-coloured fish, sometimes with huge plate-like scales. At the other end of the spectrum, some have fast-growing, dumpy fish with fewer scales.

In truth, the carp angler has never had it so good. You can select a water containing your target specimens, at a price that suits your pocket and the amount of time available. The biggest trap that many carp anglers fall into is to set their sights too high, and it's easy to get frustrated when the fishing is tough. It's better to proceed gradually and get to know tricks of the trade. This gives you the confidence to move forward and fish tougher, more sparsely stocked venues.

Most specialist carp anglers go through an apprenticeship, learning their skills on smaller, heavily stocked waters that contain singles and doubles before progressing to venues with 20-pounders and lightly stocked waters with a chance of a 30- or 40-pounder.

At the pinnacle of our sport, a band of diehard specimen hunters target individual giants on massive sheets of water over 100 acres in size. These venues might contain a mere handful of fish and it can often take several years to hook one of them. Many never do. I have great admiration for these anglers and the extraordinary efforts they invest in catching fish. Their target carp are generally 40lb plus, which even by today's standards is very high.

A short cut is to go to one of the small specialist waters that have been stocked with very big fish. These monster carp are fed on a highly nutritious diet in an attempt to maintain their weight in a fishery that could never sustain it by natural means. These waters are very popular and fulfil a demand for anglers to catch huge fish without putting in the effort required on lightly stocked, large waters. I will let you decide how they rate compared with naturally grown fish.

Another band of dedicated carp anglers love to target their quarry in running water. These river carpers prefer to achieve their goals in solitude, away from busy commercial waters. Other specialist carpers target canals and fenland drains. All these waters have produced carp over 40lb. The best carp fishing was previously confined to expensive syndicate waters, but even this has changed. Some of the best venues are open to all and the current record carp came from the Mid Kent-Fisheries, which anyone can fish.

Steady pressure prevents a
27lb carp from disappearing
behind the island on the
Elphicks North Lake in Kent.

CUNNING COMMONS

Follow the catch reports in *Angler's Mail* and you will soon realise how regularly well-known carp put in an appearance. Certain individuals are caught 30 times a year and repeat captures are an inevitable feature of the modern carp scene. On the other hand, some fish never get caught, or if they do, it's a once in a lifetime event. Strangely, many of these specimens are commons. Their refusal to pick up an angler's bait is hard to explain. Theoretically, it could be associated with a preference for a natural diet – it's almost as if they don't recognise anglers' bait as food. This theory is supported by the fact that when these fish are occasionally caught, it's on either a natural bait or a very small particle that resembles a food item found in their natural larder. These fish are the Holy Grail for the top-end specialist.

STALKING FISH

A lot of carping is focused around session angling, where anglers bivvy up at a swim for several days, hoping to attract carp into their area. This approach is usually conducted on busy waters where choice of swims is limited and the selection of bait and tactics is very critical for success.

At the other end of the scale, the opportunist or stalking approach involves carp being sought out and targeted, either singly or in groups. I think finding big fish in this way is the essence of carp fishing.

I've always found that larger carp are best targeted in areas where they are visible and at a time of year when they are most active. I concentrate my efforts

The benefits of a centrepin are clear for stalking the margin snags with a float rig. You can rotate a pin even under maximum pressure to gain vital inches of line when fishing tight to weeds and branches.

Hard earned 34lb 12oz
common taken in dour winter
conditions at Kingfisher Lake
on the Wintons Fishery in West
Sussex.

from spring to early summer and in the autumn. Big fish are obviously caught outside of these periods – most venues allow all-year-round fishing – but I like to shorten the odds in my favour.

The fantastic thing about carp is that they are willing to show themselves, and rewards are great for the angler who is prepared to do more looking than fishing. Timing varies between waters but a good starting point is dawn and dusk when light levels change very quickly. On most waters, carp love to roll, jump and, in the right conditions, cruise tantalisingly just below the surface.

Even when they can't be seen, there are plenty of clues to look for. Carp often give themselves away by sending up clouds of bubbles as they grub for food on the bottom. They also rummage through weed, reed-beds and lily pads, and can't help but make a disturbance as they push through the undergrowth. Carp are easily tracked among lilies as their foraging tugs the leaves and stalks unnaturally.

In the shallows, oily swirls and vortexes rise to the surface as water is displaced by carp fins. On pressured waters, carp might only reveal themselves at night and this is a great time to wander around quietly, listening for rolling carp as other anglers remain tucked up in their warm bivvies.

A BASIC PLAN

When opportunist fishing for carp, casting as close as possible to fish that are showing themselves is often the best strategy, providing the water isn't too deep and the carp are near the surface. Stalking fish at close-quarters is very revealing. On some waters, carp will not tolerate lines running high in the water, especially at an angle. Oddly, I've found that if the lines lie perpendicular to the bottom, carp rarely take any notice. I'm sure this is because the line mimics vertical reed stems. Often, it's a case of making sure that everything is pinned tightly to the bottom to prevent the carp becoming suspicious. Practising this tactic in the margins with fish you can see, will help when you recreate the same presentation at range.

When carp are moving, it's important to observe their direction and, if possible, intercept them. At other times, an individual fish will show itself in exactly the same place on several occasions, giving you ample opportunity to target it.

Basking carp, or fish that are cruising very close to the surface, are suckers for floating dog biscuits or crust. Groups of carp can be encouraged into feeding by a stealthy approach, resulting in several fish being taken in a short session. Solitary carp are harder to catch because there is no competitive feeding, and carefully working your bait in front of a single fish is a painstaking exercise, especially if the fish is hardly moving.

It's hot and still without a breath of wind and that inspires carp to sunbathe on top in a sheltered bay.

Being able to see the fish, taking note of weather conditions and getting to know the topography of the water are the vital keys to success. Just because a carp crashes out on the surface it doesn't mean that it's going right down to the bottom where you have cast your bait. It's important to know at what depth these fish are lying and then you can make an educated guess at how best to target them.

If carp are swimming in less than 10ft of water, they are going to be close to your hook bait and are definitely worth casting towards. If the water is 30ft deep, it's unlikely that they will be feeding on the bottom, even when they leave the surface. A suspended bait fished high in the water might be a better approach. This is especially true in winter when the bottom and surface layers of water are cold, with warmer water sandwiched between. Most of the carp will be lying in this comfort zone and it's a great time to experiment with Zig rigs at various depths to try to present a bait close to their level.

UNDERWATER CONTOURS

If there's plenty of bankside cover, a minimum of disturbance and reasonable depth, most carp patrol within a rod length of the bank. Islands and inaccessible areas, such as private banks, draw fish like magnets on busy waters, while irregularities underwater, such as gravel bars and steep drop-offs, are frequently visited by carp.

Generally, they don't like clear, open water with a uniform depth. If you are fishing a venue with few features, explore the make-up of the bottom because this could provide clues about where to present a bait. Slightly harder clay or gravel bottoms surrounded by silt usually prove productive. Natural springs clean large areas of the bottom, exposing small patches of gravel, which carp visit. Build up a mental picture of sub-surface features and this, along with actual sightings, will help you put extra carp on the bank.

A good feature-finder set-up will allow you to plot all the depths, highlight features and determine the type of bottom. I prefer braided line and an Explorer lead, which relays more feel and information than mono and a plain lead. Used with a marker or feature-finding float, you can accurately measure the depths and pinpoint potential hotspots. This is also a useful set-up on weedy venues. Many gravel pits become choked in summer, and locating small clearings where fish are showing is essential.

You can also draw fish to an area, and hold them there, by drip-feeding bait. Do this only if you have the water to yourself, or are fishing with just a few anglers. If you can make the effort, daily baiting pays dividends.

Back-winding on the Bungalows bank at day ticket Willow Park near Aldershot, as a powerful fish dives between the bars.

FORECASTING A FEEDING FRENZY

Weather conditions play a big part in carp location. In summer, wind direction and strength can influence the carp, particularly on large, open waters. Providing the wind is steady and not too changeable, your first port of call should be the windward bank, where the oxygen level is highest and carp are likely to find food. On clear venues, the backwash from strong winds stains the water for several yards out into the lake. Carp relish these conditions and, with stealth, are easily targeted just a few feet out. Low pressure, strong winds and relatively high temperatures with good cloud cover send carp into a feeding frenzy. They love these conditions and often cavort among the big waves close to the margins, around islands and especially over plateaux that rise close to the surface.

In still, warm, calm conditions with high pressure, carp cruise close to the surface or even lie static in weed-beds.

In winter, carp are usually found on the back of the wind rather than in the teeth of it. If you are standing on the bank and a chill wind makes the temperature feel sub-zero, it will have a cooling effect on the water. In these conditions, carp usually head for quieter, calmer areas of the lake where the temperature is more stable.

Some of the best winter carp fisheries are relatively shallow. The water warms up more quickly and you don't have the same layering effect of cold and warmer water where the carp feel more comfortable lying off the bottom. These shallow venues blow hot and cold depending on weather conditions. Deep waters are a nightmare in winter because the fish are hard to find and presentation is hit or miss.

This carp dived deep into the bush but Andy extricated it by wading out and exerting side-strain at close-quarters.

SMALL BOILIES

I often think carp regard boilies as a natural food. They have been used in our waters since the 1970s and have proved the most consistent carp baits of all time. Plenty of good commercial baits are available and even the most successful carp anglers rely on ready-mades. They come in several sizes and so many flavours and colours that you're spoilt for choice.

My preference is to use the smallest bait possible without being pestered by smaller fish. Carp accept smaller food items more naturally than larger ones, and the odds are stacked against them regarding the number of free offerings they pick up before finding a hook bait. For most of my carp fishing, I use 10 and 14mm diameter baits, occasionally switching to 18 and even 20mm if I need to be more selective when confronted with an abundance of tench and bream. I always reach for freezer baits as I love their consistency and find they leak a flavour trail more quickly than shelf-life boilies. Most of my carp sessions are short so this is an important factor. Shelf-life baits come into their own when you want a harder consistency, or you're fishing long sessions.

We've all got personal favourites. I'm not convinced that flavours 'blow' – in other words the carp no longer accept them. I'm still catching as many carp on Tutti Frutti boilies as I did 20 years ago. However, I do find that carp on some waters prefer sweet baits while others want savoury or fish baits, depending on the time of the year and the conditions. I normally take at least one or two alternatives and simply experiment to find what works best on the day.

BOILIE RIGS AND LINE CHOICES

I tie a hair-rig for most of my boilie fishing and favour a simple 'knotless knot' presentation. In recent seasons, I've had fantastic success with fluorocarbon as a hook-link material. Specialist braids might catch you an extra fish but I rely on casting a basic set-up into the right spot rather than flinging an elaborate rig where there are no carp.

Short-shank, wide-gape hooks suit my style of fishing with bottom baits. I vary the length of hair according to how I believe the fish are feeding. I generally start with a gap of half an inch between the bend of the hook and the top of the boilie, making it longer or shorter depending on how the session develops.

The same can be said about the length of the hook link, although it's rare for me to fish one much longer than about 9in. It's more likely to be closer to 4in., depending on the bottom make-up.

I'm a big fan of in-line, semi-fixed leger weights, which have an integral carp safety sleeve. One important piece of kit I like to use with in-line leads is a flexi-ring swivel, which allows the hook link to fold back when the weight hits the

Sweet and savoury. Tutti Fruttis and Ultra-Plex are hugely successful boilies from the Richworth range.

Flexi Ring Swivel

Illusion hook link

Arma Point SSBP (Size 10)

14mm Boile

Knotless knot hair-rig.

bottom. This keeps the hook-link knot out of the way to avoid damage, and allows the link to swing back gently towards the bottom in a natural manner. The only time I don't use in-line leads is over very soft bottoms. The lead digs in, making the hook link stand up at an angle, which I am convinced spooks carp. In this instance, I use a standard swivel leger weight with a safety lead clip.

Wherever possible I use tough fluorocarbon for the main line as well as the hook link. It sinks like a stone and takes up the bottom contours. The only disadvantage is that it is slightly stiffer than mono and so doesn't cast quite as far. For distance casting, I use a fluorocarbon shock leader and mono main line.

Pop-ups are a great alternative to a standard bottom bait, used either on their own or with a sinking boilie as a Snowman rig. For me, pop-ups come into their own on easy waters where I want something to stand out from the freebies, or when I'm fishing over weed or silt in the summer or decaying leaves and weed-beds in winter.

My standard pop-up rig is no more than a variation of my bottom rig with a slightly longer hook link and shorter hair. The pop-up is suspended between 1 and 4in. off the bottom with the aid of lead substitute putty, or Kwik Change pop-up weight.

With the Snowman rig, I like a set-up that is very slow sinking to give a soft touch down over debris or weed. It's important to keep the pop-up and the bottom bait together and I do this with a small rubber rig stop on the hair. This traps the two baits against the hair stop to eliminate the chance of the bottom bait sliding down the hair and masking the hook. To get the perfect balance, I simply snip away at the pop-up until the rig gradually starts to sink.

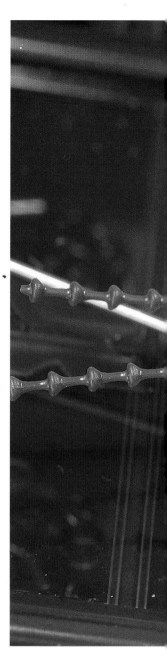

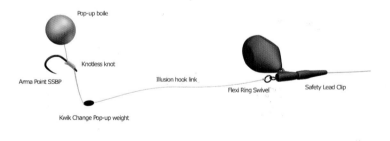

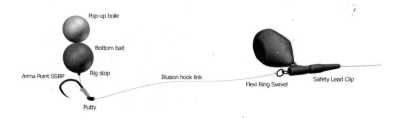

ABOVE LEFT: **Pop-up rig.**

LEFT: **Snowman rig.**

Knotless knot rig with a long hair for soft-mouthed carp. The 4in. fluorocarbon hook link is tied to a flexi-swivel ring at one end and size 10 Fox Series 1 hook at the other with a 14mm Richworth Com-Plex boilie.

PARTICLES AND HALIBUT PELLETS

Particles are a great alternative to boilies and very underrated. Unfortunately, many venues ban them, usually as a result of excessive baiting as well as bad preparation of nuts, beans and pulses. Where they are allowed, they can be extremely effective. My favourites are tigernuts, followed by maize and maple peas. Black-eyed beans and chick peas have also accounted for many fish over the years and are still worthy of consideration.

As a rule of thumb, any dehydrated particle must be soaked for at least 12 hours to rehydrate and then gently boiled for 15 minutes. Colour and flavour can be added to enhance their appeal. For some strange reason, tigernuts are consistent catchers in the coldest of weather.

Halibut pellets have made a huge impact on carp fishing. They have become almost as popular as boilies and are consistent catchers. They can be fished on the same rig as a boilie but with the addition of a pellet hair stop that wedges tightly within the drilled hole of the pellet. This ensures that the stop doesn't fall out if small fish attack the bait. Small fish can actually work the pellet off the hair. Halibut pellets are a great choice to fish with boilies – put down a bed of pellets and fish a boilie over the top.

BAITING DEVICES

It has never been so easy to introduce free offerings close to your hook bait, with baiting aids available for every conceivable requirement. For boilie baiting, many anglers still prefer throwing sticks. In the right hands, these are deadly accurate and achieve the greatest distance for individual baits. They are available in 18, 24 and 30mm diameter bores and are best used with harder, air-dried boilies because of the enormous velocity that's created with the stick.

Catapults remain the mainstay for most anglers because they are so adaptable and suit any bait. Various pouches have been designed to propel everything from single boilies to big handfuls of particles.

Spods are extremely popular and, with practise, amazingly accurate. I find them useful to bait tight holes in weed-beds. They are often used with a marker float for spot-on accuracy. Spods are probably the best implement for long-range baiting with small particles, pellets and even 'soups'. A fully loaded, large spod weighs as much as 8oz and you will need a specialist rod and heavy shock leader with a big pit reel to bait proficiently with these devices.

Hard nuts deter nuisance fish and carp love to crunch tigers in their pharyngeal teeth.

Where small amounts of freebies are needed, most anglers turn to PVA. Whether a simple stringer carrying up to six freebies is required, or one of the many types of bags, using PVA is the most effective way of putting a small mouthful of bait close to your hook bait.

Stick Rigs incorporate a thin, tubular sleeve of PVA that is filled with groundbait or a special stick mix and presented with the hook link passing through the centre of the stick. When the PVA dissolves, the fine mix of particles or groundbait lies on top of the hook link, disguising it from suspicious carp.

Network PVA bags in pineapple, maple and Activ-8 flavours, seep extra attractants around the freebies.

Fox spods with interchangeable nose cones and internal sleeves are highly versatile for different light conditions and various payloads.

FLOATER TACTICS AND TACKLE

One of the most exciting ways to catch carp is by floater fishing, a method that is greatly underexploited. On some days, carp swim close to the surface and are tricky to catch on bottom baits, but with the right approach, they are easily hooked. Wear Polaroid sunglasses to spot them. If there's more than one carp in a small area, the task is much easier. The objective is to entice the carp to feed confidently on your surface bait before casting. Dog biscuits, particularly Chum Mixers, are one of the very best floating baits. Floating trout and koi pellets will do the job but are more expensive. Many anglers believe that flavouring Mixers gives them an edge, and if it gives you extra confidence, it's worth doing. I colour my Mixers to make them easier to see and to help identify my hook bait among lots of freebies. It's rare for me to use exactly the same Mixer for free offerings as for the hook bait, unless I'm fishing at very close range and can identify individual baits.

Wherever possible, I use any wind or drift to my advantage, carefully catapulting out the freebies so they drift towards the carp. If the fish are showing at very long range, small PVA bags holding ten Mixers and a pebble for extra weight can be catapulted farther than the standard light Mixers. I make the first cast only when the fish are feeding confidently.

The best set-up is a fairly light carp rod, or even specialist floater rod, and medium-sized fixed-spool reel loaded with floating braid. It is critical to keep all of the main line floating, otherwise the rig is easily dragged out of position and will also impede the strike.

For casting weight and bite indication, I use a surface controller, for example the clear in-line Bolt Bubble, that can be semi-filled with water, or a dumpy Exocet controller. The controller float is ideal for long range because it has a large sight tip. It's also a shallow diver, making it ideal for weedy waters where there is potential for a slim-line model to dive deeply on the cast and get hung up in weed. Both these controllers can be semi-fixed and I use a small swivel to join main line to hook link. The hook link should ideally be a low-diameter floating mono. Fox Micro Plus is almost invisible on the surface and fools the wariest of carp.

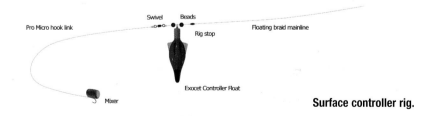

Pro Micro hook link · Swivel · Beads · Rig stop · Floating braid mainline · Exocet Controller Float · Mixer

Surface controller rig.

Soften Mixers for the hook by adding liquid flavour and colour in a plastic bag. Blow into the bag and shake them up the night before a trip.

In-line bubble floats are less prone to spook wary carp. Rubber Mixers will withstand batterings from rudd, but always takes a few crust cubes.

ATTACHING FLOATING BAIT

There are many ways of mounting your floating bait on the hook. One of the most efficient is to Superglue a single Mixer to the back of a light size 10 carp hook. Time consuming it may be, but it gives one of the best presentations of all and has accounted probably for more surface carp than anything else.

Alternatively, use a bait band for speed and convenience, but bear in mind there is always a risk of it spinning on the hook shank and masking the point. When used on the bend, the hook becomes more obvious, causing carp to shy away. Some anglers prefer very short hair-rigs and others even use elastic bands, or mount a soft Mixer on the shank of the hook itself.

Enterprise Tackle have designed a clever artificial Mixer that is counter-balanced so that the hook fishes above the bait – above the water – and therefore out of sight of the carp. I always have a few of these in my bait box.

PATIENT STRIKING

Timing the strike on the surface is sometimes extremely frustrating. Most anglers are used to relying on self-hooking rigs – on some days the fish virtually hook themselves – but most surface takes must be struck.

The most challenging moment is when a carp takes the bait with its head pointing directly at you. It's imperative that you wait until it turns away, which is easier said than done, but otherwise you will simply strike the hook from its mouth. We all get excited when a big carp sucks in the hook bait, but wait a split second and you'll hook more fish.

Catching carp on the surface at close-quarters isn't good for the blood pressure! A simple free-lined bait fished directly below the rod tip and quietly dropped in the path of a margin patroller is electric. This obviously demands a stealthy approach and a lot of patience but it's something that every carp angler should experience. The sight of those big rubbery lips slurping down your bait will stay in your mind forever.

High performance carp rods include blanks with a bonded titanium mesh like the Fox Horizon for casting extreme distances.

Advances in tempering processes have produced stronger, harder hooks with longer lasting points. Examples include the latest Arma-Point patterns from Fox offered in curved, short and long shank designs with anti-rust Teflon coatings.

Fox in-line leads are fitted with a one-piece safety sleeve so the weight pulls free and slides off if the line breaks or the rig gets snagged.

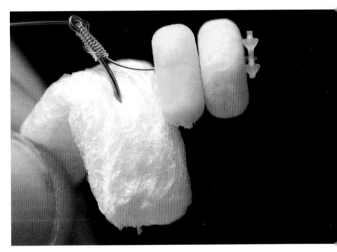

High Riser foam keeps the hook clear of debris on the descent and pops to the surface in seconds leaving a clean presentation.

STALKING RIGS FOR THE MARGINS

Another style of stalking – again a firm favourite with me – is to float fish the margins with bottom baits. The problem is that you need a float, something the majority of carp anglers don't possess, but take my advice and throw a couple in the bottom of your tackle box. At some stage in the season, an opportunity will arise to catch carp beneath your rod tip.

On most waters, carp use snags in the margins to get away from the busiest spots on the lake, and these are ideal areas for short-session stalking. Fishing in this way is sometimes like a jungle assault and not the place for 12ft rods, light lines and free-spool reels. Equip yourself with a short, powerful, specialist stalking rod of 6 to 8ft and a centrepin reel loaded with 15 or 18lb line. Centrepins allow you to retrieve vital inches of line even when the rod is under full compression, unlike fixed spools that need to be 'pumped'.

Rigs are simple. I prefer short, stubby dibber floats with bulbous bodies, rather than fine-tipped floats, because these are less prone to line bites. Often, I fish the main line straight through to a strong size 4 or 6 hook, and fix a Kwik Change pop-up weight 4in. from the hook to give the rig stability. I always use a weight that's at least twice the loading required to cock the float. It doubles up as an instant plummet to ensure that I fish at the correct depth. Occasionally, I use a hair-rigged bait but normally it's mounted directly on the hook. When I do use a hair-rig, I usually have a short hook link of similar material to the main line with a strong swivel joining the two together. This swivel is the ideal anchor

Carp stalking rig

Dibber Float

Putty over swivel

Pellet

point to add lead-substitute putty as an alternative to the Kwik Change weight.

When stalking, I bait up two or three spots with small baits such as hemp and mini pellets, in order to ensure that carp spend time rummaging around to find every last freebie. All the activity below sends up lots of vortexes and swirls to alert you to the fish's presence. A variety of hook baits produces bites. Two grains of sweetcorn or halibut pellet paste are very successful. On some waters, natural baits such as a big lobworm or a bunch of Dendrobaenas, are a better bet. Where very few nuisance fish are about, a large piece of white flake fished over a bed of dark hemp is a winning combination. This is an extremely adaptable method.

Tips down and butts up. Using twin rod rests allows you to set the rods at an acute angle, creating a more direct line towards the rigs. In strong winds, it prevents buffeting of the bow of line between rod tip and water surface. Butt Hangers with adjustable weight loadings and stainless steel chains are fitted.

On some waters, even where no signs of carp are evident, you often have a feeling that margin patrollers are around. When this is the case, I love to fish what I call a semi-static stalking approach. Although this is applicable to all types of waters, it works particularly well on small waters with relatively deep margins. I make two circuits of the lake, baiting up potential spots tight against the bank with small handfuls of freebies. A mixture of hemp, micro pellets and broken boilies is a great recipe for this approach. I select a couple of spots very close to each other, which allows me to use two rods at a time and to set a couple of traps. I use fluorocarbon right through as main line and hook link, and usually a single 14mm boilie hook bait. A 2.5oz in-line lead completes the set-up. The rods are propped on single rests rather than a pod and positioned well back from the water's edge with just the tips protruding over the margins. Then I gently lower the rigs in place, clip on a back-lead to make sure that everything is nailed down tight to the bottom, set the alarms and lightweight bobbins and sit back out of sight away from the edge of the lake to await events.

Typically, these venues don't have too much in the way of marginal snags, so I fish as light as possibly – usually 10 or 12lb line straight through matched with a through-action, 2lb 8oz test curve, 12ft carp rod.

I give each spot a couple of hours unless conditions dictate otherwise. During the course of the day, I cover a lot of water and, with any luck, land two or three decent carp. You need to be organised and travel light to get the best from this semi-mobile approach.

Line clips make it possible to hang indicators tight to the blank and help in creating a bolt rig set-up.

PODS, ALARMS AND INDICATORS

For bite indication, most anglers prefer a rod pod. I favour a Quattro pod as its goalpost buzzer bars provide a stable platform. Rear rests should be extremely secure, especially when fishing the margins, where strong, fast takes are the norm. A rubber butt grip holds the rod securely and releases quickly on the strike.

The all-singing, all-dancing electronic bite alarms give a huge range of adjustability through tone, volume and sensitivity. Remote units can be positioned close to the angler with the head sets turned down low to create the minimum of disturbance on the bank. The electronics are backed up with a visual indicator. Hanger-type systems and butt swingers are the most popular. These are low-friction models that show up dropbacks and screaming takes equally well. Pod systems give you the flexibility of two to four rod set-ups just with a change of buzzer bars.

As well as all the usual rods, reels and terminal tackle, you must have a decent landing net. Most anglers opt for a 42in. version with a Vee-style spreader block. The addition of a pontoon net float is a great aid for single-

A rigid pod without a hint of wobble: that's the Fox Quattro with its goalpost-style buzzer bars. Short-arm Butt Swinger indicators and EOS alarms complete a stable set-up.

handed landing. This ensures that the net remains on the surface, which is a huge advantage, especially in deep, sloping margins. For stalking, I prefer a 36in. model for better manoeuvrability in tight spots, and also a telescopic landing-net handle for steep banks.

Unhooking mats are compulsory on most waters and the latest generation of safety zone carp cradles provide the ultimate protection while the carp is briefly on the bank. For weighing your catch, I'm a great fan of safety weigh slings with rigid top poles that stop the weigh bag folding the carp as it is being lifted. Obviously, anything that comes into contact with the carp must be thoroughly doused with water. One final and vital piece of equipment is a pair of forceps to extract the hook efficiently.

Ideally, everything should be organised before you catch a fish but if you do get caught out, ask someone to hold your fish in the net in the margins while you get everything ready for weighing and photographing the catch.

RODS TO MEET ALL NEEDS

It's amazing how the trend towards heavier test curve rods has progressed. During most of my early carp fishing, 1.75lb carp rods were considered as stepped-up. Admittedly, we were mainly free-lining or float fishing at the time. Modern rods have to cope with much heavier leads, PVA bags, stringers and loaded Method feeders. No single rod covers all these demands and I use three models to meet my needs.

My favourite set-up is a 2.5lb test curve Fox 12ft Matrix carp rod. This has a lovely through action, which I prefer, especially for playing fish. I'm not a huge fan of fast tapered 'pokers'. The Matrix easily covers leger weights from 1 to 3oz and distances beyond 100 yards. I can use main lines from 8 to 18lb with this one rod so it's a very flexible tool. It balances out beautifully with a 10,000 size reel and copes equally well with monos and braids.

When I've got to cast huge distances to reach the fish, I use a Fox Horizon. For ultimate range, the 3.25lb test curve, 12ft 6in. model is the ultimate casting tool. I've achieved casting distances in the field measured at 180 yards with a 3.75oz weight. Realistically, 150 yards plus is possible on the lake in the right conditions with a baited hook. Lower diameter main lines and shock leaders are essential. In open water, I use 8lb line loaded to the brim on a 12,000 Big Pit sized reel with a tapered shock leader of 15 to 45lb and a 4oz casting bomb to achieve maximum range.

The other rod in my armoury is a Fox Warrior ES 12ft, 2.5lb test curve. Although this is a budget model, it has a fantastic through action for floater fishing and open-water float fishing. I've used it with line down to 6lb although it's better suited for 10 to 12lb breaking strain. With this rod I use a smaller 7000 size reel, as I'm rarely casting more than about 80 yards.

My other specialist carp rod is a Warrior Spod model. It copes with the largest spod fully loaded with bait weighing around 7oz. A tapered shock leader and braided main line on a 12,000 size reel will keep you happily baiting at distance all day long.

My career as a dedicated big-fish angler has evolved from the days when carp were my sole objective. They remain the focal point for the majority of specialists, but I'd urge any angler to broaden his horizons. I hope this book encourages you to do just that because there is immense satisfaction in becoming a true all-rounder. And if I was asked to name one over-riding priority in big-fish hunting, I'd say buy the freshest, best-quality bait available – it makes a crucial difference.

Mid-summer mirror of 22lb 8oz stalked from Hawkhurst Specimen Lake on float gear.

INDEX

Figures in italics indicate illustrations.

Angler's Mail 8, 132, 164
Avon River *36*

Bailey, Bob 28
bait boats 49, 85
bait flags 40, *41*
bait poppers 47, *47*
bait waiters *141*
baitdropper 62, *62*, 115, 116, 126,
    126, 127, 150, 151
barbel 50-69, *50*, *55*, *63*, *68*
    autumn predictability 56-7
    baits for early season 54
    catchability of monster fish 9
    feeder choices and PVA bags
        64-5, *64*
    hooks, hair-rigs and flexi-ring
        swivels 62-3, *63*
    pellets with a lollipop 58-9
    returning to the river 10
    rolling meat 65-6, *66*
    roving with rolled meat 58
    tackle choice 60-61, *60*
    using a baitdropper 62
    a vital breather 68
    weight and life expectancy 8, 52-4
barbless hooks 107
Barton Court, near Hungerford 28,
    30, *35*
beans 176
Berkshire Loddon *53*
birds, fish-eating 36
bite alarms 48-9, *48*, 186
bloodworms 150, *161*
bobbins 27, *27*, 94, 140, 151, 186
boilies 26-7, 64, *64*, 70, 74, *74*, 84,
    85, 92, *92*, 96, 126, 132, 140,
    140, 152, 174, *175*, 176, 186
bread flakes *19*, 20
breadcrust 124, 139, 140, 166
breadpunch 18, *19*, 20, 26
bream 86-97, *86*, *88*
    bite or liner? 94-7, *95*, *96*, *97*
    catchability of monster fish 9
    feeding masterplan 92, *92*, 94
    gravel pit nomads 90
    and pike 32
    spot-on casts 07
    weight and life expectancy 8, 88
Britford, Salisbury, Wiltshire *101*
buzzers 27, 94, *95*, 140, 151, 186,
    187

carp 154-89, *158*
    attaching floating bait 182, *183*
    baiting devices 176, 178, *178*,
        179
    a basic plan 166, 168

basking 166
boilie rigs and line choices 172,
    174, *174*, *175*
carp fishing venues 160, 162
carp rods 180, *183*, 188
catchability of monster fish 9
common 6, *154*, 158, 164, *165*
crucian *see* crucian carp
cunning commons 164
differentiating 158, 160
floater tactics and tackle 180, *181*
forecasting a feeding frenzy 170
king 112, 158
leather 158
Leney strain 162
life expectancy 160
mirror 158, *158*, 160
particles and halibut pellets 176,
    176
patient striking 182
pods, alarms and indicators
    186-7, *186*, *187*
and roach 22, 24
small boilies 172, *173*
stalking fish 164, 166
stalking rigs for the margins
    184-6, *184*, *185*
underwater contours 168
weight 8, 156, 160
carp dibbers 106, *106*
carp reel, Stratos *158*
Carp Society 140
casters *12*, 18, 22, 64, 74, 78, *118*,
    123, 150, 152
catapults 176
Catch 22, Lung, Norfolk *24*
centrepin *164*, 184
cheese bait 127
chub 118-33, *118*, *119*, *123*, *124*,
    132
    bait for solitary fish 126-7, *126*
    feeding tactics 122, *123*, 124
    Grand Union Canal 132
    maggots for winter 128
    magic mix 122
    returning to the river 10
    spraying maggots 132
    stillwater targets 130, *131*
    weight and spawning 8, 120
Clough, Dr Stuart 100, 102
Collingham, Nottinghamshire *64*, *68*
Colne Valley, Surrey 88
cormorants 36, *68*
corn, artificial 96, *97*
corn steep liquor 84
Cromwell Weir, Nottinghamshire *61*
crucian carp 108-117, *108*, *113*, *116*
    flexible baiting 115-16
    marginal swims 112, *113*, 114
    pole float and running line
        114-15, *115*

summer targets 112
weight and life expectancy 8, 111

dace 98-107, *99*, *101*, *102*, *104*, *107*
    barbless hooks 107
    creatures of habit 100, 102
    dibbers for fast water 106-7, *106*
    extra weight increase 8
    steady feeding 104
    weight and life expectancy 100
deadbaits: for pike 38-9, *38*
Dendrobaenas 150, 185
Derbyshire, Dean *10*, *55*
digital scales 9, 104
dinghies 49
documentation 9
dog biscuits 166, 180
Dorset Frome 100, *102*
Dorset Stour 10, *10*, *16*, *55*, *56*, *99*,
    118, 120, *132*
drifter set-up *40*, *41*
dry-fly anglers 141

echo sounders 49, 85
Elphicks North Lake, Kent *161*
Enterprise Tackle 182

Farnham, Surrey *104*
feeder rigs 26, *26*
feeders
    and barbel 64, *64*
    blockend 26, 96-7, 122
    cage *25*, 26, 96
    open-end 26, 64, 96, 97
fish welfare 10
floater fishing 180, *181*
fluorocarbon
    as a hook-link material 172
    main line *25*, 26, 42, 44, *50*, 60,
        77, 78, 174, 186
    shock leader 27, 174
Frensham Great Pond, Farnham,
    Surrey *72*, 78
Frensham Small Pond, Farnham,
    Surrey *134*, *136*, *139*, 140, *140*

Gingerbread Lake, Cambridgeshire
    44
glycerine 128
Grand Union Canal 132
Great Ouse 52
grebes 36
Greenmire Pond 120

hair-rig 172, *173*, 182, 184
halibut pellets 54, 57, *57*, 176
Hampshire Avon 100, *102*, 124
Hardwick gravel pit, Richworth Linear
    complex, Oxfordshire *131*
Harefield, Middlesex *93*
Harnham Island, Wiltshire *102*
Harrigan, Jack 58

Harris Lake, Marsh Farm, Godalming, Surrey *108*, *110*
Hawkhurst Specimen Lake, Kent *188*
hemp *12*, 18, 22, 64, 74, 78, *118*, *123*, 140, 186
Holley, Chris *118*, *132*
Hollowell Reservoir, Northamptonshire *77*, *82*
hook links, short *25*
hook technology *183*
Horseshoe Lake, Cotswolds *88*, 140, *140*, *156*

in-line leads *183*
in-line troller *41*

jerk baits 39, *39*, 47-8

kebab rig 46, *46*
Kennet River *28*, *30*, *35*, 58, 120
Kingfisher Lake, Wintons Fishery, West Sussex *165*
'knotless knot' rig 172, *175*
koi pellets 138, 180

landing net 10, 61, 186-7
leger weights 41, 140, 172, 188
lift float rig 78, *78*
line clips *186*
livebaits: for pike 38
lobworms 150, 152, 184
lollipop floats 58
London Anglers Association *101*, *102*
Longham Waterworks, Dorset *146*
lures: for pike 39, *39*

maggots
    and barbel 54, 57, 64
    and chub 128, 132
    and perch 151, 152
    and roach 26
    and rudd *134*, 140, *140*
    'wag and mag' fishing 20, 22
marker braid 27, 151
measuring length and girth 9, 10
Micorn EOS alarms *154*
Mid Kent-Fisheries 162
Milton Lake, Bury Hill Fisheries, Surrey *113*
Mole Relief Channel, Surrey *49*

New Forest Water Park, Fordingbridge *12*
nuts 176, *176*

paternoster rigs *24*, *25*, *40*, 41
    livebait 152, *152*
peacock wagglers *21*, 127
pellets 26-7, 64, 84, 96, 126, 132, *134*, 186
perch 142-53, *142*, *145*
    ambush feeders 145, 149

chopped worms and casters 150-51, *150*
colours and habits 144-6
experimenting with baits 152
long-range feeder rig 151
varied tactics 148-9, *148*, *149*
weight and life expectancy 144
pike *6*, 28-49, *28*, *30*, *33*
    ambush predators 6, 32, 36
    and bream 32
    choice of bait 38-9, *38*, *39*
    early warning bite indicators 48-9, *48*
    instant takes over hotspots 34-6, *35*, *36*
    kebab rig 46, *46*
    natural diet 32-3
    rigs for livebaiting 40-41, *40*, *41*
    rods for different methods 47-8
    spawning 35
    suspended bait 46-7, *47*
    treble positions for instant-strike rigs 42
    in trout reservoirs 30
    unhooking 32, 33
    weight and life expectancy 8, 30
    wobbling tactics and sensitive pencil rigs 42, *43*, 44, *45*
plummet 114
pole float and running line 114-15, *115*
pop-up rigs 174, *174*, 184
Puddle Chucker floats *98*
pulses 176
PVA bags 64, 178, *178*, 180, 188

record catches 10
redworms 150
river floats, low-moulded 28
roach 12-27, *12*, *15*
    baits and rigs in winter floods 18, *19*, 20
    and carp 22, 24
    catchability of monster fish 9
    competitive feeding on lakes 20, 22, *22*, *24*
    locating roach on big gravel pits 22, 24
    location 14
    pecking order within shoal 16
    returning to the river 10
    tactics for low, clear rivers 18
    tactics on gravel pits 26-7, *26*, *27*
    wariness/greed 14
    weight and life expectancy 16
Rolf's Lake, near Oxford *120*, *127*
rolling meat 65-6, *66*
Royalty Fisheries, Christchurch, Hampshire *42*, *50*, 58
rudd 134-41, *135*, *136*, *140*
    baits for cautious feeders 138-40
    dry fly fishing 141
    locating shoals 137-8

predators 138
weight 8, 136

Sabby's gravel pit, West Drayton 130
Salisbury *36*
Salisbury Avon *101*
scales 9, 10
Severn River 64
shads 149, *149*
shot: bulked around the base of the float 20, *21*
single species groups 10
Ski Lake, Cosgrove, Northants *90*
slider float 40
slider system 78-9, *78*
Snowman rig 174, *174*
solid open-end feeders *25*, 26
spods 176, *179*, 188
Sway Lakes, New Forest *15*

tape, retractable 9
tares 18
tench 70-85, *71*, *73*, *74*, *75*, *78*, *82*
    bait boats 85
    feeder tactics 84, *85*
    finding fish 76
    lift method 78, *78*
    pole rig on a long rod 81, *81*
    slider system 80-81, *80*
    specialised diet 74
    substantial gear 76-7
    weight and life expectancy 72
Thames River 64, 120, *146*, 151
Throop fisheries, Dorset Stour *56*, *128*
throwing sticks 176
treble hooks 40, *41*
Trent River *61*, 64, *64*, *67*, 68
trout pellets *154*, 180
trout reservoirs 30

unhooking mats 9, 187

'wag and mag' fishing 20, 22
Walker, Dick 144
Wareham, Dorset *102*
weigh slings 9, 187
weights and measures certificates 10
West Stow Lake, near Bury St Edmunds *6*, *158*
Wey River *59*, *104*, *145*
Willow Park, near Aldershot *169*
Wilson, Stuart *102*
Wintons fishery, Burgess Hill, West Sussex *70*, *154*, *165*
wobbling 42, *44*
worm stop buffer *142*

ACKNOWLEDGEMENTS

All photographs © Roy Westwood, except those on pages 1, 28–29, 71 and 155, which are © Greg Meenehan/Angler's Mail.
All diagrams © David Little.

Catch the
BIG ONE
every week!

Learn loads with the No.1 magazine for coarse advice.